LIVING LIKE LIVVY

By ANDRE GOVIER

Copyright © 2018 by Andre Govier

ISBN-13: 978-1984263827

ISBN-10: 198426382X

All rights reserved. No part of this publication may be reproduced, distributed, or transmitted in any form or by any means, including photo-copying, recording, or other electronic or mechanical methods, without the prior written permission of the publisher, except in the case of brief quotations embodied in critical reviews and certain other non-commercial uses permitted by copyright law. All Rights Reserved.

Dedicated to Livvy Meredith, the gift who just keeps on giving and her wonderful family who agreed to share their inspirational story for the benefit of many others. This book aims to not only raise awareness but also some much needed funds. All the royalties are being donated to fund the finding of a cure for this terrible illness.

Foreword

As a writer and a former bomb disposal operator there's a word that's becoming increasingly over-used in today's society; a word so hackneyed that it's becoming almost meaningless. It's a word we hear all the time: "Hero." And it's a shame, because it used to be such a great word! On television we're invariably bombarded with talk of athletes, celebrities and reality TV stars being heroes, but are they really? Police officers, fire fighters and members of the Armed Forces, like myself, are also classified the same way, but actually, we're all just ordinary people. Don't get me wrong, some do definitely deserve the accolade, but the fact remains that there's a big difference between public figures having a heroic moment and someone who's a true hero. In my view, it's a title that should not be given by occupation, rather by achievement. For me, A hero is someone who has given his or her life to something bigger than himself or herself, an everyday person, like a devoted parent, or even a dying child, or both. And, as I read through the pages of this book, that's exactly what I began to draw parallels with, for above all this is a book about genuine courage and true heroism.

This is the story of Olivia Meredith, a perfectly healthy girl, and her parents, who, one night in 2001, discovered that their world would change forever.

Olivia, better known as Livvy, suffered from the devastating neurological condition Rett Syndrome. This awful syndrome left Livvy physically and mentally disabled.

People with Rett syndrome have profound and multiple physical and communication disabilities and are totally reliant on others for support throughout their lives. It could occur in any family and affects approximately one in twelve thousand girls born each year. But, as the book shows, what this condition didn't damage was Livvy's spirit!

Overnight, the joyous laughter and beaming smiles of this recurrently happy little girl suddenly turned to screams and crying. Her once sparkling eyes became devoid of anything but constant fear and pain. And this was just the beginning! Three years later this remarkable little girl and her family suddenly had to face the added torment of seizures! Sometimes over one hundred seizures in a day! The dreams that all parents have for their children were destroyed in an instant! Livvy was never going to attend university, share her first kiss, fall in love, or have children of her own.

Her parents, too, were going to have to let go of the dreams they had for her and make new ones. The fear of losing her was all-consuming! In May 2005, Livvy's family nearly lost her to a severe breathing abnormality, and then, on November 7th 2008, Olivia Georgia Meredith went to sleep and never woke.

This is a story about ability more than disability. It's a story about making each second in life count. And above all, it's a story about the power of the human spirit, written by a man that the history books will most likely never mention, as he does all of this work in complete silence, and he does not want any attention or medals for what he is doing. I first met Andre Govier when we were 16 year-old recruits, sharing our first day as 'Boy Soldiers' in the British Army. From the outset he struck me as a man of integrity and we quickly became friends.

And while I'm conscious that his modesty and aforementioned integrity are the primary reasons that so little is publicly known about this brilliant author, it will come as little surprise to his readers that, behind the scenes, this modest and humble man is a committed father and husband, an active supporter of multiple charities and local community projects, and, what is perhaps less well-known, is that, since leaving the military, he has continued to devote his life to public service, working in a critical role essential to our national security. That short biography barely covers the surface, but suffice it to say, Andre is a great friend and has always been a huge inspiration to me, and for that reason, when he invited me to write this foreword, I felt instantly honoured and compelled to do so.

The fact that he has helped to raise money for Reverse Rett for six years and has committed the time and matchless writing skills to contribute 100% of the book's royalties to help raise funds to find a cure for Rett Syndrome, is testament to the qualities of this truly inspirational man.

This book will make you laugh, cry and feel inspired. It will remind you that in the ordinary world, there are some extraordinary people. But the real heroes do things because they're the right things to do.

Maj (Ret'd) Chris Hunter QGM

Former Bomb Disposal Operator and Best-selling Author of "Eight Lives Down" and "Extreme Risk"

London, United Kingdom

Contents

Chapter 1

As winter turned into spring during 1999, life was going brilliantly. I had been blessed with two beautiful daughters who were both happy and healthy, while also having the most loving, caring and hardworking husband in Alan, who was not only a truly awesome support, role model and best friend, but also a great father. Our family lived in a charming village called New Invention, within the Walsall area of the English West Midlands. It was situated only four miles west of the major city, Wolverhampton, but still retained the charm and quiet attributes of an English village. New Invention, while often feeling remote, contained more than the basics required for a happy home life with its green open spaces, the Wyrley and Essington Canal and Sneyd Reservoir, developed to provide water to the locks of the former Wyrley branch of the canal and Rough Wood Nature Reserve. There was a lovely village school, medical centre, dentists, libraries and a small shopping centre.

Alan, my husband had worked installing new windows into homes and businesses since the age of sixteen. He had plenty of work, but sadly this often meant he had to work extremely long hours, sometimes toiling seven days a week. Despite this, he always made sure the girls and I were the centre of his life, and he loved doing all the jobs a modern young father should do with his daughters. The eldest, Kennedy, born in 1996 was three years old in the spring of this year. She was a happy, loving but slightly mischievous little mummy's girl, who worshipped a purple dinosaur called Barney. Kennedy followed me everywhere. She was such good company, but even at the age of three hated being on her own at night. We would often lay her down to sleep at bedtime and she would be as good as gold, but come one o'clock in the morning I'd find Kennedy snuggled up next to me in our bed, hoping we wouldn't notice she'd sneaked in! Eden was my second daughter, born in the later part of 1997. She has been a very happy child and even at eighteen months old she was incredibly content and happy in her own company. As long as she had her drink of milk she would be quite happy watching television on her own, or entertaining herself with toys, puzzling out life's mysteries by herself.

Having worked, firstly as a production assistant in a factory and later doing office work in a surveyor's, I had taken the decision to give up work and become a full-time mum, not only to my daughters Kennedy and Eden but also to the latest, due to arrive in the first half of May 1999. Everything seemed perfect, or as perfect as it was going to be at this time. We lived a world away from the issues filling the news headlines outside our quiet village. The papers were full of the awful homophobic hate bombings around London's Soho district at this time, but all my focus was on preparing for the soon to arrive new addition about to join our family.

I had a good relationship with both my parents, and an excellent group of friends with whom to socialise. My mum, Diane, was a great support, to be called upon when needed, and, although she had separated from my Dad, Phil, he remained a very proud if not always a hands-on granddad. My dad loved the girls and would come to our house each weekend without fail. He was always so excited to see them, although there were some jobs he had not been willing to assist with. There is still a family story going around that when I myself had been a baby, each time my nappy needed changing he would pick me up in a panic and rush me to his sister's house, asking her to change my nappy, which thankfully she would be happy to do!

My mum, Diane, was a great nan to Kennedy and Eden, and very excited about the arrival of the new baby. We would often talk, and she was a much-needed support, not only in an emotional way, but also at any time I needed help or somebody to watch the girls at short notice.

During my first two pregnancies, I had on both occasions gone into premature labour and had severe blood loss through haemorrhaging. For this reason, I'd been strongly advised against my preferred option, which was a home birth. The doctors at my local hospital were very insistent that this baby must be born in a maternity ward. I was in no position to argue. This third pregnancy had been relatively straight forward with no huge complications. I endured a few months of nausea, which was just put down to morning sickness. This had also been the case during my previous two pregnancies, but I had no concerns of dramatic weight loss or other problems. Everything seemed to be going well. On the evening of Tuesday, 4th May 1999, when the rest of the country was settling down to watch their favourite evening soap operas on TV, my labour started and I knew this was it! Alan helped me into our black Mk 3 Ford Escort and drove us the short three mile journey to Walsall Manor Hospital, leaving family to look after Kennedy and Eden. Alan was just as excited for this baby as he had been for our first child. The evening passed into night and we reached early morning. The pain, as expected, began to increase. I'd been told many times, I had hours to go. Knowing I was going to be in pain for a long time, I'd chosen the option of having an epidural to relieve the agony. The midwife wasn't sympathetic to the pain, and just kept saying, "You have hours left." She was still saying this at 6 o'clock the next morning. When the anaesthetist walked in, all gowned up ready to give me the much needed pain relief in my spine, he noticed the agony I was in, and was quick to question the midwife's estimated time of delivery, requesting another examination. She begrudgingly had another look, and realised I was very much in the final stages of labour and that it was now too late for the epidural to be administered. Less than thirty minutes later, at 0653 hrs on 5th May 1999, our beautiful Olivia Meredith was born into this world, weighing a healthy 7 lbs and 7 ounces (3.4 kilogrammes). We would call her Livvy for short.

Everything seemed as it should be. Tests were done on skin tone, breathing, reflex response, heart rate and muscle tone. All tests were passed without any concerns and a perfect mark was achieved on the Apgar Score. Livvy had passed her first test with ease. Alan was excited and bursting with smiles as he quickly made phone calls telling family our news of Livvy's arrival into the world.

The only concern the hospital raised with Livvy was her strong reflux. She was being sick, bringing much of the milk she was given straight back up. The hospital wanted Livvy to be bottle fed rather than breast fed naturally. This would allow us to measure how much milk she was taking in. I'd no huge concerns. I felt completely exhausted, I was just eager to get home and start being a family again, together with our new baby. I couldn't do this quite yet, because the doctors on Walsall Manor Maternity Ward wanted to monitor Livvy for twenty-four hours just to be certain the sickness caused by the reflux wasn't going to be a serious cause for concern. I had to settle instead for a lovely visit from Kennedy and Eden coming to see me on the ward, and introducing them to their new baby sister for the first time.

On Thursday morning, doctors gave Livvy the all clear to go home. Alan collected us both for the long-awaited short drive home. Livvy was now keeping sufficient milk down. I wasn't feeling too well in myself, but at the time I thought this was due to the ordeal of having given birth. I felt so weak, exhausted and tired. I didn't remember feeling quite so weak after giving birth to Kennedy or Eden.

Two days later, as Saturday 7th May arrived, I was feeling terrible! My mum, Diane, visited and realised my temperature was through the roof and I was almost passing out with exhaustion. She was straight on the phone to the doctor, insisting he come immediately to the house. He attended promptly, and my only memory was being rushed back to the hospital by ambulance. The assumption was that my illness was due to the pregnancy, so I had to go straight to the maternity ward again at Walsall Manor Hospital. Here I was diagnosed with the infectious superbug condition MRSA. (Methicillin-Resistant Staphylococcus Aureus.) The nurses were quick to isolate me straight into quarantine, to reduce the risk of a further spread of this nasty bug. I was not isolated enough that I couldn't hear the constant sounds of babies crying, and this was a cruel reminder that I was not with my own new born baby. This was a real torment, and I hated not being able to spend those first few days being able to hold my baby, as other mothers a short distance away were able to do. Even my family were not permitted to visit, except for Alan, and even he was allowed only one visit. Although I was not fully with it and conscious, due to the illness, I remember seeing my husband in scrubs, gown and a mask as he entered my private room to see how I was getting on. I was not well enough for much talking, but I remember being made aware that my dad Phil was also at the hospital, demanding to see me, but being denied access. He was extremely cross and frustrated about not having an opportunity to check on me, as he was due to fly away on holiday to America the next day. Dad was saying, "If I don't get to see her I am not going on this holiday." He did his best to gain access but in the end, he had to fly off on holiday having been denied his visit. In those days there were no paternity payments, and Alan still had to work hours and often he would have long travelling times. He would get

Kennedy, Eden and Livvy in the car and drop them off at my mum's house before shooting off to spend a day fitting windows. He had a lot to cope with for a fella. Added to this was the fact he also felt my pain of not being able to hold my new baby or either of my other girls.

When Friday14th May came, I was starting to feel just a little bit better, although still very weak. I'd come through the worst of it. The constant sounds of new mothers in the adjacent bays enjoying their first few hours with their new babies was starting to become an unbearable torture. Kennedy and Eden were due to be bridesmaids at a family wedding the next day, and I was determined to show I was now well enough to go home. Late into the evening a doctor agreed to my discharge. I was taken home by Alan. There was no way I was going to miss seeing my girls, being bridesmaids for the first time! I felt so happy to get home and give them each a massive hug, and then I got what sleep I could.

The next morning, I helped dress the girls, and Alan drove us on the nine mile journey to Dudley for the Wedding of his mum, Brenda, to her new husband, Chris. It was an enjoyable day and the girls looked absolutely gorgeous! I was so pleased I went. I couldn't have missed this for the world! All seemed to go so smoothly, up until the photographs, when I realised I was passing out once more. While the photographs were being taken, I was being held up by the groom, Chris. "Sorry Chris."

After the trauma of this first week, life with Livvy soon became relatively normal. She had her cot bed in our bedroom and she slept as well as any new born baby could be expected to. Alan was a star, doing more than his share of the feeds and nappy changes through the night, despite having to be ready to leave the house for work at 7 o'clock each morning. He would always do the last feed of the night in the bedroom silently, allowing me to sleep on. Livvy still had a bad reflux and she brought back much of the milk she would drink. This, unfortunately, meant that, day or night, Livvy often needed a quick bath, to get clean again after each feed. Alan never complained, but instead just kept being what a great dad and husband should be. After doing this he would then leave to work twelve hours outside in rain, wind or shine fitting windows, and still come home exhausted but happy to take up dad duties.

I enjoyed these months, though. Kennedy was going to playgroup, and soon after, Eden was also. I met loads of new friends and became part of a nice little community who would often meet up for a bite of lunch or a good old chat. My mum, Diane, and dad, Phil, were regular callers, and nothing indicated to me that anything was wrong. This was life and we were enjoying it as families should. I wish these months could have lasted a bit longer.

Chapter 2

One day, at the end of February 2001, at about lunch time, everything changed. Livvy was now twenty-one months old. Alan was at work and my older girls, Kennedy and Eden, were still at nursery. Livvy just screamed! She continued to scream and then scream some more. Nothing I could do would calm her down! She was just sitting on the living room floor. At first, I thought she was just having an almighty temper tantrum, but the screaming was pure rage for no obvious reason. When this had gone on for what felt like hours, and nothing I could do would settle her, I became more and more worried. She would just scream and scream and scream. The only break would be when she was forced to stop for breath, and then she would start up all over again! There was no break in it. I recall at one point I had to just put her down in her cot for five minutes and let her scream there, because I needed a little break myself. I felt so baffled and kept checking her all over, thinking she might have hurt herself, but I could find nothing. I was convinced she must have hurt herself, but there was nothing to be seen anywhere on her body, or movements which might give me a clue. That day was one long series of piercing screams, and, sadly, the first of many.

Livvy had always had a severe reflux and, as a small baby, she had lots of colic-type pain. I then thought this might be something similar, but the rage and the level of screaming were very different. When she had colic as a baby, we could hug her and she would happily lay on your

15

arms and be soothed. With this screaming there was no soothing. I tried hugging, watching her favourite TV programs and much more but each failed to make any difference to the constant rage.

None of this was helped by the fact I was now in the very final stages of pregnancy with my fourth daughter, Brodie. I had already gone past the due date, and had an appointment to be induced at Walsall Manor Hospital, on the following Tuesday. Also, on the day when this happened, Alan came home from work tired and not looking quite his normal happy self. He listened kindly to how my day had been, and I explained about all the screaming and rage and how I just couldn't do anything to settle Livvy. Alan smiled and said "Ok, I've just lost my job today." I couldn't believe it! Things were hard already with three girls and a fourth one due any moment, and we were already struggling to pay the mortgage on the house. This was a big shock! Alan explained that when he'd asked his boss at the glass company if he could have next Tuesday off to watch the birth of his fourth daughter, the reaction had been getting the boot. They basically said, "You can have the day off and every day after that and don't bother coming back." The boss had not even had the courage or decency to say this himself, but sent his foreman to do his dirty work for him. There are some extremely mean-spirited people in this world and, knowing Alans's situation, the boss at the glass company sits high on the list of these. He was a spoilt little boy who just loved bossing he minions about while on a crazy power trip. He resented Alan having a day off to see his child being born!

I was already mentally exhausted and this was a real low point while we came to terms with how uncertain our future looked from this evening onwards. Alan has never been shy of work and had a good reputation. Luckily, he received two offers of similar work within two days.

We quickly managed to get some tests arranged for Livvy at the hospital. They looked at her severe reflux, and this didn't appear to be causing the screaming. They also tried to check her ears and test her hearing. Unfortunately, they couldn't test either very well, because Livvy just wasn't responding. She just ignored everything that they tried to get her to do. This was a world away from only a few weeks ago, when Livvy had quite unexpectedly decided to crawl up the stairs at home! The stairs in our house go half way up and then turn back on themselves. Livvy had managed the first half with Alan just behind her, checking she was safe. He was ever so proud of her for this. We now appeared to have a different child!

The screaming was awful! Because this, I just couldn't go anywhere. I remember one day I took her to visit my mum, Diane. Livvy loved going to her nanny's but on this day Nanny had moved some furniture around. Livvy took one look at this and she just couldn't cope! It was just as if someone had hurt her! She just screamed and screamed! It was because she had gone to Nanny's and it just wasn't how it should be in her head. She was absolutely devastated! In the end, all I could do was pack up and bring Livvy home.

For a very short time, and it was only a few days, things seemed to get a bit better again. I was not sure why, maybe the screaming was a little bit quieter or maybe it was because I had given birth to Brodie and we were all happy.

Livvy took to her little sister quite well. There was an issue with strollers. (Pushchairs) Every time I put Livvy close to Brodie she would try to kiss, bite or scratch her. She was always trying to get at her. She was trying to hug her rather than be aggressive. Livvy loved dolls, and she just wanted to hold and hug Brodie like a doll.

This screaming didn't just go on for six weeks, but happened every morning, noon and night for much longer than that. She would wake up screaming and still be screaming when she was put to bed. People kept telling me that I had spoilt her and it was all my fault. I knew that wasn't the reason and this was something much worse. I knew it was not a behaviour thing, I just didn't know what it was. This was the reaction I was getting from lots of people. I do fully understand them coming to this conclusion, because, if you were to see her, you would have just thought she was having a temper tantrum. I knew it wasn't. This isn't Livvy. She was normally full of joy. Nothing bothered her. I knew something was going on. I kept going back to the doctors and kept trying to get more hearing tests, but no answers were offered.

The doctor referred her to a consultant. They were still only focusing on the reflux as an explanation. I knew it was nothing to do with this. I knew it had to be something much more. It was starting to feel as if I was banging my head against a brick wall! I asked "Where has her walking gone? Where has her talking gone? Where has the eye contact gone? She used to be so joyful and now…"

All the doctor could answer was "urm urm urm" before suggesting this was because of a new baby being in the house and it was jealousy. She was very nice and listened to me, but she could offer no answers. I think they also thought Livvy's issues were behaviour rather than illness. We were sent to see the paediatrician at Walsall Manor Hospital, who didn't seem to realise how severe her reflux was. I remember having to sit with the paediatrician and literally feed her so she would vomit all over, to get her attention, so she would realise I wasn't talking about a little bit of colic.

I didn't know why she was screaming constantly. I felt that I was having to make up explanations all the time, and I was apologising constantly for her behaviour when I knew it wasn't just behaviour. I didn't really have a clue what it was. At times I just felt like saying "Livvy, why are you doing this to me?"

This was such a terrible period for me. In a short period of time I felt as if I had lost a huge part of Livvy. I had also lost several friends who had no idea, or just weren't interested. Some stopped asking me out, or, with others, I felt I couldn't take Livvy to visit any more. While this was ongoing, we had the stress of paying the mortgage, caused by the short period when Alan had been between jobs.

At the same time as the constant screaming had started another observation was made. This was perhaps a larger clue of what was to come. Livvy also started constantly wringing her hands and rubbing them together. She had gone from having good gross motor skills with her hands to just rubbing them together. I can only describe this as being similar to the character Fagin in the way he kept rubbing his hands in the film Oliver Twist. It was there, a huge clue, very early on, although it was the screaming that caught our attention first. Her thumbs took the worst of it. She would constantly rub her thumbs over one another.

I used to have a good group of friends who were mainly the parents of other children at the nursery. We used to meet up and let the kids play in the Wacky Warehouse. On some visits, Livvy's screaming or stealing food may have been hard for them to deal with or understand. I felt awkward about going, and sometimes declined invites. I soon stopped being asked to go altogether. I can't be sure if this was because they didn't know what to do with Livvy's screaming or perhaps I had just said "No" too many times. Whatever the reason, I'd lost touch and friendship with other mums. It became obvious in the conversations on the way to school with other mums that I just wasn't there. They were doing everything without me, and it was as if I didn't exist anymore. I became very insular at this point. I soon realized, that, not only was I no longer being invited anywhere, but the friends who used to call on the phone every day, also started to call less, and then stopped calling altogether.

Sometimes, when Livvy was screaming, the only thing I could do was drive. I remember the times we would get in the car and just drive. Brodie would be in one car seat and Livvy would be in another. I would put the radio on because the movement and the music would start to calm her a little. We are a family of country music fans, so naturally Livvy also liked country music. Olivia loved listening to Reba McEntire and Trisha Yearwood. We didn't go to any favourite places, we didn't just go a couple of miles. We would just drive for hours and then drive some more. We'd go and visit Alan, wherever he was working, fitting windows on a site or at a house. This could be over thirty miles away. I just needed some sanity. At these moments when she had fallen asleep in the car, I had, if only for a brief time, just a little bit of much needed sanity!

It wasn't just the screaming which was taking my sanity. Livvy would be on a constant mission to destroy or put anything in her mouth! She would go into the bin all the time, and, if I'd left anything out, Livvy would pull it apart. She almost had a constant need to eat. Everything had to be put in her mouth. If I was changing Brodie's nappy and I was not quick enough picking it up, then I'd see Livvy have it across the floor in a flash. If Kennedy and Eden had something to eat and left any, then Livvy would be into it. We had to put a stairgate across the kitchen door. I had found her in the rubbish bin eating teabags. On a different day, Alan heard a shrieking, and came into the living room to find Livvy holding the kitten in the air by its tail. The poor little thing! Livvy had no concept she was hurting it and the kitten just became one of many items we had to safeguard from Livvy. She loved the kitten but couldn't be left alone with any animals.

Alan had a younger sister called Lorna who lived in nearby Wednesfield with her boyfriend David, who would later go on to become her husband. One Halloween, we all went over with the girls to have some quality family time socialising. They had been warned to make the house "Livvy proof", before we set off. Unfortunately, they had forgotten one item. David had left his parents' following a row. He had not spoken or had contact with them since. The only possession he had taken from his home was an ornamental dragon. He was not only very fond of this dragon, but this was highly sentimental being the only possession he still owned to remind him of his entire childhood. Livvy went straight up to it, while we grownups were talking two feet away, and bashed it. That was the end of that! The dragon was smashed to pieces! David must have been distraught, but he made no issue about it. He joined the ever-growing group of people, who were prepared to let Livvy get away with murder. It was very hard to be cross with a child who is laughing. "Sorry David."

There was one defining moment when I did realise I would not be visiting many people's houses again. I had a good friend called Nicky. She was trying so hard to be supportive and understanding. I was so pleased to be going out to visit and to be accepted when many were no longer calling. I contacted Nicky before I went, asking her to move everything out of the way that Livvy might get hold of. She didn't mind moving the cat food and the dog food, because Livvy had been into these things previously. Despite this, Nicky was still inviting me back. One time she had invited us round and told me she'd had a new hall carpet fitted, which was a cream in a light shade. Nicky and I were sitting chatting and Livvy was aimlessly walking in a circle out of the living room door and back in the dining room and around and around in a circle. She was constantly doing this whilst I enjoyed a chat with Nicky. She was happy walking in a circle, so I let her just keep walking. Suddenly, Livvy walked into the living room with a teabag. My friend had made a cup of tea and left this on the side. Livvy had picked this up and ripped it up in her mouth and spread it all over Nicky's new cream carpet. I was mortified! Nicky did not make a big deal of this and said, "No it's fine, don't worry I can clean it up."

Inside I knew that this was the last invite I'd be accepting to come back here. To be fair to Nicky, she did invite me around again, but I just didn't feel able to go after the latest incident, although Nicky had a lovely house and Kennedy and Nicky's son were good friends. When I came home I could have cried. I was devastated! I felt I had to apologise for everything all the time. Livvy was literally into everything!

I took all my girls to nursery from an early age. I wanted them to have the social interaction. I did stop taking Livvy, now nearly three years old, for a while because all she was doing while there was scream. After the screaming had ended I started taking Livvy to playgroup. She would never play with anything. She would just be walking around aimlessly picking things up and dropping them. The problems began when Livvy started taking other children's toast. She was just obsessed by food! These other children were small toddlers who would then get upset. They would go running to their parents upset because Livvy has taken their food and I would have to go and apologise. I would have to apologise again and again and again. Then would come the looks from the parents who are saying "You need to keep that child under control. She has her own toast. Why does she need other peoples?"

I just got tired of explaining, because I had no answers as to why. Why was she taking other people's toast when her toast is in the bowl in front of her? I was just lost for any logical reason! The other problem was that she had gone from being a child who would listen to me and interact with me, to a child who just didn't pay attention when I was trying to tell her off. It now appeared she was just lost! I just kept trying to be as normal as possible, while at the same time not knowing what the hell was going on. She had lost any ability to interact with me. It felt as if she couldn't see or hear me while I was trying to talk to her. Livvy had fallen into her own little world!

Just prior to the screaming starting, Livvy was beginning to talk, or at least make babbling sounds with meaning. She would go "Dad Dad Dad," and "Mom Mom Mom," and "Dee Dee Dee," for Kennedy. Now there was nothing. She had, prior to the screaming, had the normal eighteen months assessment with regards her development. The only thing picked up was that she had been a little late in starting to walk, but Livvy had passed all other tests with good scores. They were happy with her starting to talk, the building with blocks and putting shapes into the right holes.

With Livvy having gone from normal behaviour to screaming and not communicating, it was hard to puzzle out why. We had no computer to search on. I was completely without a clue as to why this was happening. Some people kept mentioning autism to me. This can set in at about the age of two or three years. I was a little naïve, and really had very little idea about the world of disability. I knew nothing, and I was literally clambering anywhere and everywhere for advice. Some professionals were still saying it was her hearing. They thought she was screaming because she could not hear herself. They also said she was ignoring me because she couldn't hear me. They later changed their minds and said it was not the hearing and suggested we visit the Child Development Centre at Shelfield.

I continued the quest to find out what was wrong and causing her such distress. I felt so frustrated, even when turning up at the Child Development Centre, because I still did not have any idea what it was they were looking for. I had the same question running through my head and nobody appeared able to give me any answers.

The Church certainly never gave me any. As a family, going to our local Methodist Church each Sunday played a big part in our lives. Kennedy and Eden went to Girls' Brigade. Livvy would get very excited by the music and singing in church, and in her own way she would sing along also. The only difference was that she was just screaming to the music rather than singing. She was also a lot louder than anybody else! One Sunday, when we had all been to church as a family together, I was approached by one of the church elders. She quite bluntly suggested, that I should not bring her to church anymore. What was I to think now? This was another of those moments which really felt like the last straw to me. Nobody wanted this child and now, not even God wanted her. I now really couldn't go anywhere. I remember that awful journey home, thinking that if this is what Christianity means, then I don't want anything to do with it. A very long time passed before I would ever go near that church again! I made the decision to walk away from the church, but not from God. This was a place in which I hoped to find peace and solitude, but, instead, all I found was judgement. With all this going on, I found myself almost at breaking point. Now with this cruel blow, it seemed that the church members prepared to push me over the edge without a second thought or ounce of compassion. I was physically exhausted, emotionally in despair and I hadn't got one ounce of fight left in me. The church members were very straight laced. They liked children to turn up, go to Sunday school and not be heard again, and Livvy couldn't go there. In hindsight, I now just think they were old people who thought she was being naughty. Maybe if I had known the facts and been able to explain that she had a disability, there would have been a different response, but the reality was that, at this point in time, I did not have a clue what was going on with Livvy.

In hindsight, one reason why, my friends might have left me was, perhaps that their children were now full time at school and I still had a baby and a toddler, and the toddler was just screaming. There was no malice in it, it was just that my world was changing and none of them really knew why either, or how to reach me, as I became more isolated. I would describe my state now as purely survival mode. If I was invited to go somewhere, I didn't think I would have either the energy or the inclination to go, due not only to the constant screaming, but also because she would make herself sick all over the place through screaming.

This was the story of my whole 2001! Things were being made worse by the fact that Alan was working not only long hours, but also a long way away. He was travelling two hours each day to St Helen's, fitting windows and getting back after 9 o'clock each night, and he would always be exhausted! I was needing him at home with me as things were getting harder and harder. We moved home away from New Invention, as we were also finding it harder and harder to pay the mortgage. Instead of risking repossession, we decided to sell and, after a brief period living with family, we managed to get a house in Little Bloxwich. This is a small rural area on the north side of Walsall, which was relatively modern with all its homes having been built since the Second World War.

It was soon after leaving New Invention that we got a call for Livvy to go for a fourteen-day assessment at the Child Development Centre at Shelfield. This was because, after the most recent attempt at a hearing test, the decision had been made that Livvy had some sort of learning disability. Here they were going to do assessments on her behaviour and her development. This was for ten days of testing, over two weeks.

I set off on the ten-minute drive to Shelfield in the Black Ford Escort while Kennedy and Eden were at school. My mum, Diane, looked after Brodie, and Alan was working away still doing long hours. I was full of hope that this assessment would bring some answers, but, at the same time, I had no idea just what it was they were looking for. At this point the screaming had all but stopped, and Livvy had dropped into her own little world. The screaming had robbed her of her eye contact and her words, and even the ability to pay any interest in anything. There was a time when we didn't exist in Livvy's life. She would just wander around aimlessly on her own. She would pick up anything and drop it. You couldn't take your eyes off her for one second! I recall one day at this point, at my mum's house, when she even picked up dog muck! We also caught her eating a packet of her granddad's cigarettes! This was Trevor, my mum's husband and my stepfather. I'm not sure he was impressed. "Sorry Trevor."

The staff at the Child Development Centre were amazing! It was also good to see her next to other children of her own age. It was also clear to see, there was a massive difference between them and her. We could see in the other children that many had obvious disabilities, but Livvy was still really very different. The staff would do a whole series of different activities and tests with Livvy. She would always just ignore them and walk off. We would keep going after her and trying to bring her back. After one of the sessions, early in this assessment, I remember, as I was leaving, the staff asked, "Can you bring your husband with you tomorrow? "

I said "Of course, but why? If you have something to say can you please just say it!"

"We would rather speak to you and your husband," they answered. "We think Livvy has a Global Learning Disability."

"Is that what you were going to tell us? I don't need my husband here to be told this. I just need to know," I said. At this point I was just desperate for answers! I was actually relieved to hear this, although I didn't really know what it was. My questions now were, "What's next? What do I do? How can I help her?" I still couldn't get my head around the fact she had walked and talked previously. They never had any answers to that. Every time I asked that question to experts I just got a look of pity. People just seemed to feel sorry for me, but nobody gave me the answers. We were told she was going to be behind and she would develop a bit more slowly than other children. No mention was made of anything more long term.

It was arranged that she would have some early years teaching and some physiotherapy, and everything seemed to just start happening. She would be assessed for Disability Living Allowance. The money would certainly help, although it was not a huge amount. I was being handed lots of forms to fill in, but still no answers. While the diagnosis was not correct, this was a turning point. Now she had been officially diagnosed with a condition, then suddenly I had professionals coming up with suggestions to make life better. I had some hope after months when all I had known was despair. The staff were as helpful as they could be and I appreciated all they did.

Livvy had a specialist teacher who came to try work to recover her gross motor skills in her hands. This change of attitude and assistance changed everything. I had some useful advice and things to do. I had something to 100% focus on. I just wanted to bring back the little girl I had lost. If they showed me an exercise to work on, I would work my hardest on that exercise, doing it as often as I could or as often as Livvy would allow.

We then started the assessments for schooling. I remember the heart-breaking conversation of being told she would never be in any mainstream school but would have to attend a special needs school. They asked, "How do you feel about that?"

It was a lot to take in, but on the scale of what was going on, I didn't really care. So long as she was happy at school, then I didn't mind. A team of specialist helpers was soon available and helping Livvy. This included a physiotherapist and also an early years specialist. Livvy still had some walking ability, but she had a weird walk. She was due to be starting at nursery as she was now three years old. They started the process of getting Livvy statemented for school.

Livvy was still being very sick at this stage and needing baths during the day and night.

My mum, Diane, was an immense help to me during this period. She would come and look after Livvy when I needed her. It is fair to say that as soon as Livvy had been diagnosed my mum became her champion. If Livvy was in hospital, my mum would be there. If Livvy needed to do building blocks, then she would do building blocks with her. If she was upset and needed to go for a walk, my mum would have Livvy in the stroller in a flash and be walking her.

Alan was still having to work very hard and long hours while we were doing our best with Livvy. My side of the family was my lifeline seven days a week. My younger sister, Lyndsey, would come to the house for hours and help. She would amuse all the kids and keep them entertained, giving me great support. She was still young herself, and in school, but she still kept coming around to help me. My younger brother, Richard, would also come and amuse the kids. When I had lived in New Invention, it had been too far for them to visit regularly, but now we'd moved closer, they were able to call as often as they liked after their day at school.

Life was looking a little better. We had some professional help, and my family support was kicking in. I did remember all the people who, prior to diagnosis, had kept blaming me for Livvy's screaming, people who said she was naughty and accused me of having spoilt her. Not one of these finger pointers would ever later apologise!

As there were three other girls in the house, there was a set routine to our day, although I wouldn't describe it as regimented. So long as Livvy got her food at meal times she was quite happy. She would sometimes stay up to see her dad return from work, but more often than not she would fall asleep on the sofa, or even with her head in the toybox! We'd made many changes to the house. We used to call it "Livvy proofing." If I was going to visit my mum, then I would have to call ahead and say, "Livvy proof your house." If not, ornaments would go flying! I had no ornaments in my house anymore. When we moved into our latest house, I hadn't unpacked half the stuff, because I knew there was no point. It was only after we'd moved that we started to receive Disability Living Allowance for Livvy. This, while not a fortune, was greatly appreciated and it made life a little easier.

Everybody likes to be in control of his or her life. The screaming months had made my life anything but controlled. Now, with the physiotherapy, early years, the extra money and fantastic help from my mum, Lyndsey and Richard, I had a bit of control back in my life, instead of feeling sick with fear most of the time. I had four children who depended on me and I was conscious that all of my smiles, for a long time, had been fake ones.

Livvy still had some, albeit limited, walking ability, and also a fantastic talent for trashing anything she could put her hands on! She was, however, in her own way, content after the screaming ended. Livvy had found her own peace. She would still aimlessly walk in circles but also settle to watch some TV. Compared to how things were, Livvy was almost a happy child. She knew what she liked and the things she disliked. She knew which music she liked, which TV programmes and also which people. She loved her little sister, Brodie, and, as a pair, they were like two peas in a pod. She was still snatching toys and grabbing any food she could. She would sometimes look up and make eye contact with us. It was slight, but a tiny glint in her eye was back once more.

Chapter 3

Things were finally starting to take a positive turn, and we were looking at schools for Livvy. We were lucky to have two excellent special schools in close proximity. We looked at Old Hall Special School in Walsall. This seemed a good and well-equipped school, which appeared more than able to deal with the most complex needs. We also paid a visit to Oakwood Special School. This was such a nice school. It had such a welcoming warmth and caring atmosphere about it. Oakwood had all the characteristics of a well-run village school. While still being a special school, it did not feel in any way like a clinical environment. It was small and friendly with about eighty pupils. The headteacher here, Kay Mills, was a wonderful woman! She was in her mid-forties, efficient but kind, professional but understanding. But most of all she had a positive and bubbly persona. Kay Mills's friendly and warm welcome immediately instilled confidence in me that this was the place for Livvy. Kay Mills had an inspirational ethos for the school which was "Every child has potential and every child is an individual." Kay Mills ran a school which was never going to be about what our child can't do, but more about what she can do. Many of the things Livvy did in this school were like things other four-year olds did in mainstream schools. She would enjoy listening to stories and watching children's television programmes. They did lots of play acting in school and used costumes to learn about history. One week she might be a queen, the next week she might be a Tudor lady. They also did baking with the children, and Livvy enjoyed music therapy. She loved music in school! The children could play with instruments. Livvy loved tambourines and drums, along with anything she could make a loud noise with! In a bizarre way, making a loud noise with instruments was very calming for Livvy. While Livvy still enjoyed her own space at times, and often wanted to be alone, at Oakwood she started to mix with other children and she made some dear friends. She would have the school dinner provided at school rather than taking a packed lunch. These were fairly standard meals similar to those served in other schools. Livvy was still obsessed by food, so this was maybe her favourite part of the school day. In traditional Livvy fashion, she would eat her own meal with a little assistance from the staff with a spoon or fork. As soon as she had finished she would try, and often succeed in, taking other children's food. She needed assistance in eating her own meal, but when it came to eating somebody else's food, Livvy needed no assistance whatsoever!

For the first year, I would take Livvy on the short journey to school each day myself. The Black Ford Escort had now been replaced and I loved our new car, which was a green Seat Alhambra people carrier. We now needed a much larger vehicle and this had space for seven people. It was much better suited for transporting Livvy. We had to get a car which separated Livvy from anybody sitting next to her. She would literally attack anybody sitting next to her, in a loving way. She meant no harm with her version of tough love, but we couldn't have her sitting next to little Brodie! This was Livvy's way of showing affection. Whilst Livvy had a chair to ride in, at the time she started school she had still managed to retain some of her walking ability. For just over a year she was still able to walk into school from the car without any need to ride in her chair. Life at this stage, compared to earlier, was good. Livvy was happy, her sisters were happy, Alan was always in steady work still fitting windows, and I could breathe without fear again. All this was about to change dramatically again soon.

Early one evening we were all at home together as a family watching the bedtime hour on TV. Livvy had not been quite herself all day, and was resting on my lap. She suddenly started to thrust and shake and, while her eyes were open and she was clearly conscious, she was not really with us as we sat in shock. She was not breathing normally. This was a huge seizure! This felt as if it went on for ages, but it was probably only a minute. I was so scared, not having a clue what was happening now. She was just shaking and shaking and shaking! The shaking was from top to bottom, and quite violent. I had never seen a seizure before, and just panicked with fear while Alan rang for an ambulance.

At hospital, the doctors were not able to give us any explanation for this sudden and very violent seizure. They came up with words such as "infant convulsion," but no explanation. On the evening Livvy went to hospital, she had twenty-six seizures before midnight. The next day she had one hundred and six seizures and still we couldn't get anything resembling an explanation from the doctors. Poor

Livvy was now out of it as she was absolutely exhausted. Luckily, the later seizures on the second day were a bit less violent, and more just blacking out. Livvy was just out of it. She would go into a seizure and wake up. She would try and get up but go into another seizure. It was just horrendous and heart-breaking seeing her try to come back to normal and rise but going straight down on her back. Livvy was put into a private room and was still having seizure after seizure while they were examining her at the hospital. Various doctors would come and see her and all they could do was scratch their heads seeking answers while each tried best to guess a probable cause. When somebody has epilepsy, they will have one seizure and maybe another one, but with this they just couldn't understand the build-up of one after another continuously. They started doing tests, but no answers were coming. These were just happening, and each time without any warning. The first seizure had shocked the life out of me, but by the time they were almost constant on the second day I felt numb. Sometimes, as soon as one seizure had ended, the next one would start. These days seemed to go on forever. It was not only a point of feeling as if we had absolutely no control but for a very long time we also got no answers. They did say that children with special needs do have epilepsy, or maybe she had an epilepsy condition. They would mention a couple of possible syndromes which could cause epilepsy, but none would give this level of seizures, and at no point did they mention Rett Syndrome. The normal reaction to this would be to panic. At the first seizure, I did panic, but, as these were just going on and on, while we were seriously concerned, there was no time to panic. We were working constantly trying to keep her happy and comfortable, so we just didn't have any spare energy or time to waste panicking. If we were not doing this, then we were begging the doctors to find answers. These hellish days felt as if they went on for ever, but in reality, they only lasted for about nine weeks. They were, however, the most physically and emotionally exhausting nine weeks you could imagine, not only for all of us, but especially for Livvy. At one point, it did feel as if we had left home and moved onto the hospital ward to live. We were there all the time, just trying to do anything we could. Sometimes, with gritted teeth or a forced smile, it was a never-ending battle against this still unknown enemy, which just wasn't going to give us a break!

The doctors started to treat Livvy with a drug called Tegretol and other anti-epilepsy medicines, which Livvy would have to take orally. Doctors attempted to put a drip into Livvy for her medicines, but Livvy was not having any of that. She was a nightmare with a cannula in her arm! Some of the seizures were better described as absences rather than fits. She would turn blue whilst having these. The drugs would dope her up, so we had to come to a decision and this was to put up with a few seizures and have Livvy awake. It was not an easy job to find the balance of just the right amount of medication to give Livvy some life, but also not have her suffering constant seizures.

We still were not getting any credible explanation for the large number of seizures. The doctors were telling us that children with special needs would often get epilepsy, but they had no idea why it was at this level. We had no idea either. Through sheer desperation I now started to do some research of my own. I needed to learn what was causing this. I put some of the symptoms into Google on my desktop computer at home and found a page which listed the signs of Rett Syndrome.

• Slowed growth. Smaller than normal head size (microcephaly) is usually the first sign that a child has Rett Syndrome

• Loss of normal movement and coordination. The first signs often include reduced hand control and a decreasing ability to crawl or walk normally. Loss of previously gained milestones in gross motor or fine motor skills

• Loss of communication abilities. Children with Rett Syndrome typically begin to lose the ability to speak, to make eye contact and to communicate in other ways. They may become disinterested in other people, toys and their surroundings. Some children have rapid changes, such as a sudden loss of speech. Over time, most children gradually regain eye contact and develop non-verbal communication skills.

• Abnormal hand movements. Children with Rett Syndrome typically develop repetitive, purposeless hand movements that may differ for each person. Hand movements may include hand wringing, squeezing, clapping, tapping or rubbing.

• Unusual eye movements. Children with Rett Syndrome tend to have unusual eye movements, such as intense staring, blinking, crossed eyes or closing one eye at a time.

• Breathing problems. These include breath-holding, abnormally rapid breathing (hyperventilation), forceful exhalation of air or saliva, and swallowing air. These problems tend to occur during waking hours, but not during sleep.

• Agitation and irritability. Children with Rett Syndrome become increasingly agitated and irritable as they get older. Periods of crying or screaming may begin suddenly, for no apparent reason, and last for hours.

•   Other abnormal behaviours. These may include, for example, sudden, odd facial expressions and long bouts of laughter, hand licking, and grasping of hair or clothing.

•   Cognitive disabilities. Loss of skills can be accompanied by a loss of intellectual functioning.

•   Seizures. Most people who have Rett Syndrome experience seizures at some time during their lives.

I felt numb. Whilst I had been desperate to look for an explanation of what might be wrong with Livvy, I looked at the information about Rett Syndrome and said, "I don't want that one. I really don't want that one." I did search further, but nothing that I could find seemed similar.

Livvy had all but one of these signs. From what I could see she had a normal size head. There was nothing wrong with the size of her head. Maybe she did not have Rett Syndrome. I convinced myself that she couldn't have Rett, because her head was a normal size and it was there in black and white that girls with Rett had smaller heads. This was the lifeline I clung to. She hadn't got that! I don't want that one! I also thought that if she had this condition, a doctor would have already said something about it.

I mentioned it to my husband Alan, who had a bit more faith in the doctors than I did. I don't think he appreciated me looking and thought I was making myself ill. He said that if that was the condition she had, the doctors would have identified it by now. Alan had complete faith in the medical professionals, and by this time I had lost all faith. He kept saying that, if this was what Livvy had, the doctors would have found it by now.

My faith had crashed, because when the seizures started the doctors should have had answers, but they didn't. Sometimes they came out with things that they should not have done. Alan had accepted their explanation that she had Global Learning Disability, with Epilepsy, but I couldn't accept it. For me there was something more. Looking back, I knew at this point it was Rett Syndrome, but I desperately didn't want it to be and my heart was not ready to accept that it was.

I never discussed this with professionals. I was already being treated like the neurotic parent who wouldn't accept what she was being told and was constantly wanting more answers. I thought that, if I told them I had googled something, I would be laughed out of the hospital. They had already put a label on me, as somebody who wouldn't accept what she was being told and didn't listen and kept asking questions. They didn't believe me when I told them she had previously been able to talk and walk and now she no longer had the ability to do either. They did not listen to my questions, so the chances of getting answers was nil. One doctor said to my face "Mrs Meredith, you have got to let this go. You are becoming neurotic about it." Another doctor, who was a registrar at the hospital, suggested that I actually wanted there to be more to it than just Global Learning Difficulty with Epilepsy. A registrar is a doctor who had undergone advanced training in a specialist field of medicine in order eventually to become a consultant. Of course I didn't want there to be more! I just knew that, deep down, there had to be something more to explain what I was seeing. This doctor was not a "people person" and he didn't have the answers I was after. Sadly, he reacted badly to me asking. I wish that he had listened to me also, in the same way he kept insisting I was not listening to him. The registrar said, "Mrs Meredith you have two bright children, but you seem unable to accept that this one will not be as clever."

I replied "I don't give a shit about her academic ability. I just want to know why she is having a hundred seizures a day!" In hindsight, I must have driven them mad. I was the woman who just wanted to know why, why, why, and they had no answers to give me!

Eventually, after many weeks, the drugs controlled the seizures and Livvy did get well enough to return to school. The seizures had stolen all that was left of Livvy's walking, but it was good to leave the hospital environment. We had regular visits in school from the community paediatrician, who would see Livvy and talk about her progress and treatments at school. He was one of those doctors that some people loved and some people hated, but

I always loved Doctor Carter, because he was always very honest. All I ever wanted was honesty. If a doctor tells me what it is, then I can prepare and deal with it, but doctors who tell me nothing I find hard to deal with.

One day he came into school and we were having a long discussion about her epilepsy and her falling out of bed. Livvy was sitting there doing her stereotypical hand movements and he asked, "Have you ever heard of a condition called Rett Syndrome?" My heart sank and I explained that I had seen and read about it.

Dr Carter then said, "I'm a hundred percent certain that Livvy has Rett Syndrome."

After months of desperately wanting to hear answers my first thought was, "I don't want to hear this! I don't want that one!" My worst fears were coming true. There was another girl in the school who also had Rett Syndrome, so I knew I was at least sitting with a doctor who actually knew what it was. Dr Carter phoned Birmingham Children's Hospital and arranged an appointment with a consultant neurologist.

He understood and fully believed our story about how Livvy had developed normally. He also understood about the loss of functions and the screaming, and it all made total sense. I knew I hadn't been going mad. I left the school and remember just getting in the car and driving to Alan, who was with colleagues working on a job fitting windows. I said, "I need to speak to you." I couldn't speak but instead just cried. After much crying, I did manage to explain what I had just learned. Alan said "Ok, we need to learn as much about Rett as we can. We need to learn how to deal with it and do our best, just as we have done with everything else."

I could only say "Alan, I didn't want that one." I felt sorry for Alan, as here he was ten minutes from the school. I had turned up at his job after he had just taken somebody's windows out. I was a blubbering mess and Livvy was in the car. He had to console me and he was obviously very upset himself. As soon as we calmed down enough to leave, Alan had to put somebody's new windows back in.

The following week we travelled to Birmingham Children's Hospital. It was here that blood tests were taken in order to do the MECP2 gene test, and it was here that we got the clinical diagnosis. This was all done in one appointment. We saw a Mr Phillips, who was one of the top neurologists in Birmingham. Mr Phillips was amazing, not only because he was an incredible doctor, but he was also very honest. They did look at her medication and make some changes. It felt good that now, for the first time, we were having medications prescribed at the same time as actually knowing what it was we were medicating her for. Previously it had just felt as if Livvy was the guinea pig, whose health was totally dependent on the guesswork of others. The thing I remember about Mr Phillips was that he wanted to meet Livvy and he wanted to know her full history. He also knew and understood the stages she had gone through. There was no looking at me suggesting I was a neurotic mother.

There was patience and a genuine feeling not only of caring, but also wanting to help, not only Livvy, but also us, by explaining things and answering some of the questions we had so desperately tried to have answered previously. The only dark moment I do remember from this meeting was when Mr Phillips measured Livvy's head. This, sadly, confirmed that Livvy's head was a little smaller than it should be at her age. My heart sank through the floor. When I had previously looked at the ten signs of Rett Syndrome, she had only nine, to my mind. The thought that her head had been the correct size was my last lifeline of hope. This also had just been taken away. It felt so final and devastating to have the last seed of hope taken away. For a while I just couldn't stop crying. Her head was not abnormal, but it was smaller than it should be.

Mr Phillips talked about the regression. Livvy had developed Rett Syndrome slightly later than many, and she had walked and talked prior to becoming ill. It was due to the amount of walking and talking she had been able to do that her regression had been so severe. If she had developed Rett Syndrome a few months earlier, the levels of screaming and seizures would possibly have been less intense. Every case of Rett is different, but they also all have some similarities. Livvy had developed a bit more than many girls before the Rett Symptoms brought chaos, confusion and worry on a huge scale. Mr Phillips, while being sympathetic and understanding, also took great care not to offer false hope. I remember him just looking at me and saying, "I can't promise you forever." I know that at this time Rett

Syndrome research was very new, but the knowledge Mr Phillips gave was very ahead of that of many others. Many children, I later found out, also got wrongly diagnosed, with conditions such as Cerebral Palsy or similar. Here, for the first time, we had found somebody who fully understood and wasn't just scratching his head and guessing. He explained to us the condition fully. It might seem odd, but, when he did this, I also felt a little relief, as I knew that I hadn't cracked up. In an odd way, while the last couple of years had been far from normal, having spent time talking with Mr Phillips I now realised that, for a Rett girl, this was normal. It was a relief to have a professional who believed all we were saying. I told him about how many times I had tried talking to different doctors about what had been going on, and, while they had listened, nobody had really heard me. He looked at me and said, "I hear you now."

At the same time as hearing the worst news possible, I had suddenly found a person who totally understood and was both capable and keen to offer the help, support and answers I had been desperately craving. In a weird way, the Rett Syndrome diagnosis was a relief.

Alan and I left the hospital and put Livvy in the back of the car. We just sat in the front and broke down in tears. It was the first time we had been left alone. Alan got extremely emotional and hit the steering wheel very hard. Livvy started giggling. She then giggled and laughed some more. She found the whole situation hilarious and just giggled her head off. Alan and I looked at each other and agreed that whilst this was a diagnosis, it was not her. We had a big choice with two options to make' and to make now. We could either become consumed by the diagnosis or we could remember that Livvy was still our Livvy. This wasn't going to change who she was.

Next came the task of telling people about Livvy's latest news. Nobody I spoke to, or knew, had ever heard of Rett Syndrome. I learned later that her school knew a bit about it as another child there, called Rachel, also had Rett. Livvy had been best friends with Rachel from day one. They were like two peas in a pod and I later often wondered, if they both knew they had Rett Syndrome before we did. I only found out about Rachel after I had told the school about the Rett diagnosis. Rachel's parents also thought the girls both knew about the Rett before we did.

Other than Rachel's parents and staff at the school, nobody we spoke to had heard of Rett Syndrome. The most common response I would get from people was, "She doesn't swear, she doesn't swear." Of course, they were confusing the condition of Tourette's (A neurological condition which can cause constant swearing and twitching) with Rett Syndrome. If I only had a pound for each time I'd had to explain that one!

I had always been aware of lots of people turning and staring when I was out with Livvy, and, soon after the diagnosis, I think I went through a stage of telling every single person I encountered. I remember one day being in the local big supermarket and a lady was looking at Livvy in her chair when she was hand wringing. She came over and said, "Ah she's so sweet. What does she have?"

I said, "She's got the condition called Rett Syndrome." Looking surprised she looked us both in the eye and then said, "Oh is that the one where they swear and shout?"

"No, that's Tourette's," I informed her.

"Oh, I've never heard of Rett Syndrome," she said. I then explained it as best as I could at that point. This was an almost scripted conversation I repeated over and over from this point onwards. It did slightly frustrate me that nobody ever seemed to have heard of Rett Syndrome, but I certainly couldn't blame them because, until recently, I hadn't either! I do know that life would have been made slightly easier if people had known about her condition, and, by this, I don't just mean doctors, but the public as a whole. There were a few people, such as Livvy's grandparents, who did their own research so that they didn't have to keep asking Alan and me the questions, but, besides them, and staff at Livvy's school, everybody else was oblivious to the existence of Rett Syndrome!

One thing I also learned quickly was that not everybody's journey with Rett was the same. I promptly started having conversations with the mother of Rachel, Livvy's friend at school who also had Rett. She was called Sue, and she was very surprised to hear that Livvy had the same condition as her daughter. Rachel had never reached the walking stage and her talking had been very limited before Rett took hold. As a result, her regression was not as major or dramatic as Livvy's had been, with less screaming and not as many seizures. The condition is caused by the mutation of the MCEP2 gene, but the mutations can be different. Some girls may be able to walk a little bit and even talk just a little bit. Mr Phillips told us that Livvy had one of the most severe cases, and she had lost everything. I would have loved to have more time to study and find out about the science behind Rett, but now I was totally focused on looking after Livvy and also my three other daughters. There was no hope of any cure mentioned at this time, and it would be a few more years to come before any signs of a hope or serious talk of a cure would emerge.

My sisters Cara and Lyndsey, and my mum Diane, kept me going and still came around, helping to amuse Livvy and watch her for me. I didn't want to leave her, so often, wherever I was going, they would always come with me and bring Livvy. Even if just popping out to the shops, I would still bring Livvy along.

The treatment or therapies Livvy was having had changed little from before to after getting the diagnosis. What had changed, and did give us a boost, was having an answer. We now understood what was going on, and why. It was not quite the frightening rollercoaster of the unknown we had endured prior to diagnosis, when we were not given a huge amount of advice or ideas for doing things.

The attitude of the school didn't change, and the head teacher, Kay Mills, still pressed her marvellous ethos that 'Every child is an individual and every child has potential.' They used Makaton sign language at the school to communicate with some of the children and this was also used and encouraged with Livvy. Kay was such a supportive and caring teacher. I cannot really praise her enough for her levels of care and enthusiasm for giving these kids the best she could! I was one of those mums who would keep their child off school if they thought she was going to have a seizure. Kay would ring me and say "You need to send her into school. She needs to see her friends. If there's a problem, I promise I will phone you. You have to trust us and you cannot do this on your own. Get her here every day. If she is going to live her life with seizures, then we are going to have to learn to deal with it as well." This was her attitude from day one. It was maybe the little shake I needed back then, because I just wanted to keep Livvy with me constantly, which would not have been the best thing for her development. Kay said "Listen to me, Sara, you are just going to make yourself ill and Livvy deserves to be in school. A lot of our kids have seizures. That is why we are a special needs school. We are geared up." This lady was not only so practical, but also so right and utterly brilliant!

Kay said "You send her into school and if she is ill then I will send her home. I will promise you this but you must bring her into school. What is the difference between her having a seizure stuck at home or having a seizure with her friends playing? If you don't bring her in then she is going to miss the good bits of life."

It was this great school that helped us get a little bit of Livvy back again. She left us totally during the screaming stage and it took about six months before we got any of her back again. It wasn't the same Livvy, but a little of her did return. She certainly had moments when we saw the mischievous smile again. Before the seizures, she was walking around aimlessly, but some of Livvy definitely came back! Once she started this school, Livvy did start to make some connections straight away. Her friend Rachel was having to use a wheelchair before Livvy, so if they were doing any activity, Livvy would always have to sit next to Rachel. Livvy would also fall out with another friend, called Nicole, over a boy they both wanted to sit next to. Little special moments which many parents could perhaps take for granted, for us were rare and precious glimpses of normal interaction other kids enjoy all day and every day.

The seizures consumed Livvy again, totally for a while. But once they were being medicated we had to make a decision. We could stop her having seizures but lose our interaction with her all the time, or we could decide to put up with some seizures, but have Livvy "with us" for some of the day. This is what we decided was the better of two bad choices. We couldn't imagine her sleeping throughout the entire day!

Now that we had a diagnosis for Livvy, and the medication was giving some relief from the very high number of seizures, with the wonderful support from school, the end of 2004 was almost starting to feel normal. Once more I could breathe and manage life for Livvy and my three other wonderful girls. Christmas shopping was all but complete, and on the evening of 23rd December 2004 things took another step for the worse. We had recently had a new addition to the family, a lovely Golden Labrador puppy called Angel. I decided to take Angel for a walk down to the nearby Canal in Walsall Wood. It was only about 6 o'clock in the evening, but very dark due to the time of year. I followed Angel under a bridge on the canal. In the darkness under the bridge there was a group of six or seven teenage lads. I didn't like the way they were looking at me, and thought to myself, "Here we go." I had been looking at my phone, and was just putting it away. It was a very cheap phone with no special attributes, but these lads had decided they wanted it. At first, I said "No, you're not having it." They became more menacing, so I ended up saying "Ok, have it, I don't care," and gave them my phone. These males were either very drunk or '"high" on some substance. They were being really rowdy, and then one of them tripped me up, which they all thought was hilarious. Every time I tried to get up another one would push me back down. This was followed by several kicks to the stomach. It was humiliation, pain and terror all at the same time! It felt as if they all had to have a go. I was in the foetal position. It felt as though they were all putting kicks in, with most of them aimed at my front. Thankfully, they were either disturbed or got bored, and I heard "Come on let's leave her there," before they all took off, running away. A man was coming down the canal at this time, and he had found my dog. Soon after, he found me, in a state. I don't know who this man was. I wish I did, because I would love to thank him one day. I did manage to get up, but was in pain. I was really embarrassed also. I had always been one of those people who would say, "I'm not scared of kids." Here I was having taken a kicking under a dark bridge by a group of fifteen to seventeen year-olds. I knew one of them, or at least knew his family. Every area has a couple of families that everybody knows. He was part of our local problem family that everybody knew.

I got the dog and managed some brief words of thanks before stumbling home. I told Alan what had just happened, while I was still crying and upset, but I was also trying not to scare the girls, who were all still quite young. Alan called the police, who came to the house, took a statement and sent units to try and find this gang of lads. This was without success. I assume that by this time they had already dispersed. We tried ringing my phone number, which was no longer ringing out. I explained to the officers that I knew one and possibly two of the lads, and they said that these boys were well known to them, and that the incident sounded typical of the sort of behaviour they were known for. They asked what we wanted from them in this situation. The reality was that one of my daughters went to school with a sister from this family. To pursue this would be putting her in a tough and awkward situation. If I had prosecuted, firstly I would have to prove it was them anyway. Secondly, they were kids, so they would probably only get a smack on the hand and they couldn't give a crap about the law anyway. Thirdly, my girls would have to put up with the fallout. We only lived just around the corner from this family. I wasn't going to let Kennedy or Eden be exposed to that, so I decided I wouldn't be taking it any further. All I kept thinking was that this was my own stupid fault for walking the dog alone in the dark.

I was feeling very silly, and I was also in severe pain throughout all Christmas day of 2004. I had some bruising, but nothing huge. On Boxing Day, I went to my mother in law Brenda's house. I didn't know if I had moved wrongly, or what had happened, but I was now totally doubled up in pain. I attempted to lay down on a bed, but the levels of pain were so bad that I couldn't even lay down. It was just pure agony! I did finally pass out with the pain, so an ambulance was called. I was taken to the closest hospital, which was Sandwell General Hospital. After a long time waiting around here, the hospital staff said that I just had a water infection. (Also known as a urinary tract infection.) They sent me home. Alan did explain how I had recently been quite badly beaten, but they stuck to their diagnosis, and quickly sent me home, feeling stupid for having wasted everybody's time. The pain did not go away. It just continued. I felt unwell, but wasn't going to be pulled down by a water infection. One day I remember standing at the top of the stairs. The next minute I was at the bottom, wondering how I'd got there! The pain was causing blackouts! I rang Alan, and explained that I had just blacked out and didn't know how. These moments of blacking out and collapsing happened numerous times. Alan suggested that I might be overtired and needing more rest. When it happened again, I made an appointment to see my own doctor. The doctor wasn't sure why I was blacking out and collapsing and suggested I might have a form of epilepsy. He added me on to a waiting list for an appointment to see a neurologist. The wait to see the neurologist was thirteen weeks, so Alan paid for me to see one privately.

The neurologist didn't think it was epilepsy, but a combination of me having so much going on in my life while also still suffering extreme pain following the kicking under the bridge. Every now and again my body was just shutting down. I was struggling to get out of bed. I was only just coping with doing the journeys to school and to playgroup and was having to go straight back to bed. If anything, my pain and fatigue were constantly getting worse and not better.

Just as I was getting weaker and even more tired, Livvy also took a turn for the worse and developed abnormal breathing. She was straight back in hospital. She was struggling to breath and now, each time she had a seizure, Livvy was turning blue! In April 2005, a doctor on the ward decided that, due to this, Livvy now needed to be ventilated. She needed a machine to do the breathing for her. He also told us that there was little more they could do for Livvy. We were taken to the Intensive Care Ward at Walsall Manor Hospital so that Livvy could be anaesthetised in order to be ventilated. What would normally happen is that they would ventilate the child on the normal Intensive Care and then move her to a children's Intensive Care. This was like the final nail in the coffin for Alan working. He knew I just couldn't do this anymore. We had taken Livvy into hospital, just thinking that this was another bout of bad seizures. We would get it sorted out, and maybe have to get her medication adjusted. In hospital they gave her a strong drug due to her breathing problems, but because of her epilepsy this drug caused her to crash. This was the point at which the doctor said that she needed to be rushed to intensive care. Once here, an anaesthetist turned up. He was blonde with long hair and could only be described as a surfer dude. Livvy was still just awake when he turned up and as soon as she took one look at him she started giggling. She still had an eye for somebody she thought looked cute, and she was smiling and fluttering her eyes at this young man, who'd come to put her to sleep. People think things like this don't happen, but this really did! He refused to ventilate her until she absolutely needed to be. He said, "I am not ventilating a giggling child." Livvy's personality was still very much alive! She may have been a very ill little girl, but she had thoughts and funny mischievous ideas still going on behind those pretty eyes, no matter how ill she was. Even when struggling to breathe, Livvy still had the energy to smile at someone she thought looked cute! We all spent a long, worrying night on Intensive Care, just to be sent back to the ward the very next day.

The next day on the ward Livvy was still having seizures and breathing problems and the doctor had no answers. Eventually he called the Palliative Care team. He said "I'm very sorry, but this is all we can do. Now it is just about saying your goodbyes." This was a totally horrific time. I could not accept this! I would not accept this! As quickly as possible we got everybody there. They, like me, were all distraught and couldn't believe what was happening! They appeared to have given up on her!

I received a phone call from my friend Sue. She was the lady who also had a daughter with Rett, called Rachel, at the same school Livvy attended. I told her what was happening. She worked at Birmingham Children's Hospital. She took it upon herself to find our neurologist in Birmingham and update him. He demanded Livvy be taken immediately to Birmingham Children's Hospital. He said that, at present, her treatment was being badly mismanaged and that she needed to be transferred straight away. He sent transport from Birmingham to collect Livvy, to speed up the transfer, and off we went. This all happened so fast! As Livvy and I shot through to Birmingham, all my family also followed behind because they had been told they would be saying their goodbyes. Walsall Manor Hospital staff had said that there was nothing more that could be done."

When we arrived at Birmingham, nurses and doctors got to work straight away. A doctor came and spoke to us saying, "She is very ill, but we do not need all the family here saying goodbye, at least not right now. There are still treatments we can do." They set to work. It was not plain sailing by any stretch. She had a further episode of not breathing and had to be resuscitated with chest compressions. The medical staff worked very hard. I can only describe what they did as incredible! The atmosphere within forty-eight hours had totally changed, and we were no longer all doom and gloom. From this point on we got a little control.

Alan returned to work after being off while Livvy was so ill. There was a mountain of jobs that needed doing at home. Things had mounted up while we had been at the hospital, always wondering if Livvy was going to live or die. I was still in terrible pain. I didn't know if I could drive because the pain was still so chronic. Alan said, "I don't know if I can keep doing this."

He told his boss, who had been so good to him, that he wanted to be at home looking after his family. His present boss was not only very understanding and supportive, but he had always made sure Alan had plenty of work. He'd picked up on how hard Alan was finding it to be in two places at once. He told him that his priority needed to be his family right now. He told Alan that the firm was letting him go, and sacked him! Whilst getting sacked again might seem a bit harsh, this time it was a sign of great kindness. It was obvious Alan couldn't carry on working. He was fired for the reason that he could then immediately go and claim benefits. If he had voluntarily left his job, he would have received nothing to live off. Alan would have needed to wait for several weeks before getting a penny. The company whose staff were so understanding, and sacked Alan, because it was the right decision for him and his family, was Select Windows. These people were wonderful to us at a time when we needed all the help we could get. This was the best company Alan ever worked for. He was really respected and totally supported. If he needed to disappear because Livvy was having a seizure or another drama, there was never any hassle. This company was a great employer. It's a strange comparison that I am mentioning two window companies sacking Alan, in very different circumstances. The manager at Alan's previous job fitting Glass was thoughtless and cruel and showed no understanding when Alan wanted to be present at the birth of his child and yet at Select Windows Alan was respected, valued and cared for. He was sacked because it was the best thing for him and his family.

Chapter 4

We were now a family living on benefits through no fault of our own. Things were tight, and we had very little money to get by, but at the same time a massive weight was lifted. Having Alan at home was a huge relief. When I thought about what was worth the most, having Alan at home to help me with the girls, while I was still so ill, was great! Many things had to change. We stopped going away, and each pound had to be spent wisely. It was nice having Alan there. It was the backup I'd really needed. In 2005 we had to say "No" to the girls a few times. We were not a family who had enjoyed having a lot of money previously, but being on benefits in 2005 gave us some difficult moments financially. Alan and I were not drinkers or smokers, and I couldn't recall when I had last bought myself any new clothing. We also had to stop the girls going to clubs and having dance classes, because we just couldn't afford these any more.

During this time, my own health was still going downhill. The assault had left me sore, but I was getting more and more ill. I was undergoing lots of investigative tests, and I was stuck in bed ill for a long time during this year. At first the doctors diagnosed me with ME. (Often referred to as Chronic Fatigue Syndrome.) Many months later it was diagnosed as Fibromyalgia, this due to the pain I felt pain all over, and extreme muscle stiffness. I was told that it can often start following a traumatic event, which might have been the event by the canal, but it could have equally been caused by the MRSA I had following Livvy's birth. My immune system was in bits, and I couldn't manage Livvy on my own. Most of the time I was laid up in bed, and, if I did need to leave the house, it was only possible with the use of crutches. Little did I know, when I was first laid up with this crippling fatigue and pain that it was going to last for many years. I still have this pain today.

After Livvy had been officially diagnosed with Rett Syndrome, we started doing some research, and found the small number of charities available to help. One we found was Rett UK, and we heard that there was a conference in Harrogate to provide information and advice for families of girls with Rett Syndrome. We couldn't afford the hotel, so we managed to stop with my mum and stepdad who were staying in a caravan, just outside Scarborough. (A caravan is a type of mobile home.) My mum looked after the other girls while Alan, Livvy and I drove to Harrogate to spend the day at the conference. The conference was in a hotel which not only had no changing facilities, but was also only equipped with just one tiny little lift! Not exactly ideal as a location to host a conference with over forty girls who had Rett Syndrome, and their families! It was only a one-day event with an evening meal at the end. Due to our situation, we only attended the conference, because we just didn't have spare cash for hotel meals. If I had money for such luxury, I would always have a bill which would need that cash more, or an item the girls needed for school. Alan and I both went to the conference full of hope. We hoped to make new friends and contacts, hoped to get some advice and support and pick up some useful information which would make life a bit easier. What we got was something quite different!

When the conference started, we all entered a large room. Alan and I were totally overwhelmed to see so many other girls who also had Rett. We could see also, that many families knew each other. There was a community here. We were not alone. This should have been a greatly reassuring experience, meeting other who had been through similar traumas and learning how to deal with different issues. The reality was that we were even more terrified and frightened! Livvy was having a very bad period of strong and regular seizures. As we looked around the room most of the other girls all seemed quite calm. They were not causing constant chaos. It felt to me as if, while my little girl shared this condition with the others in the room, she was having by far the worst seizures and was far more ill on this day. That might sound an awful thing to say, but the reality of the day was that, while we were there, Livvy spent almost the entire day having fits and turning blue. She kept us both busy, and we didn't get to take in much of what was being said to us. No matter how much we wanted to take the info in, the entire day became background noise, as Livvy was having seizures and stopping breathing, while whatever was being offered missed us completely. I didn't even know at that time that the stoppage of breathing was a normal part of Rett. Alan and I both left at the end of the day feeling that little had been achieved. We hadn't even been able to afford to stay and have the meal with the other families. All the expectations we had of making steps in the right direction came to nothing. Soon after I saw the Rett UK Newsletter / Leaflet which covered the event. There were lots of photographs of the other girls with Rett. They all had all been dressed up with their hair looking nice, and each had been made to look pretty for the camera. It felt very painful that there were none of Livvy. She had missed out. I know she was having a lot of fits, but it would have been nice to have just one picture of her. I felt so deflated that I moved away from the Rett UK Charity, as I felt it just didn't have anything to offer me. For sure this Charity did help some people, but I felt a need to distance myself as it was doing nothing for me. When living on benefits and looking after a child with complex needs, you can't afford financially or emotionally to have great hopes and expectations turn to disappointment too often.

(To be clear this is not the Reverse Rett Charity with which I became involved later and to which the royalties from this book shall be donated.)

?

Chapter 5

Despite the disappointment of Harrogate, one thing did change for the better following the diagnosis. There was a full and determined effort to get Livvy's medication right. We didn't want her asleep all the time, while at the same time we also needed to control the number of seizures. Alan and I also had three other daughters to look after, and they wanted to do stuff and enjoy life the way every other kid does. They didn't ask for the world, and they knew that funds were always low, but they all wanted, and deserved, to do the things all normal kids do.

The medication Livvy was on affected the carotene levels in her body, so the doctors recommended we give her some specific foods. So I remember buying Livvy an avocado. I remember chopping it for her to eat one morning. It was horrible and slimy, and I was thinking to myself 'Please don't like this!" Of course, she loved it, and from that day onwards Livvy had to have an avocado every day before school!

When talking about days out and activities, we had a rule that we would never say "We can't do that," because of Livvy. Instead we would always say "How shall we?" We were not going to be prevented from having fun and developing because of our situation. However, we did sometimes have to be creative in order to make things happen. No girl, and certainly no girl of mine, was going to be deprived of a fun experience if I could help it, just because of a wheelchair, or fear of a seizure. "How shall we?" became a bit of a family motto, and we said it, a lot.

It was with this mind-set that we, as a family, set off to the Cumbrian Lake District, to go and do some activities. All the girls were maybe a little scared when they saw a huge cliff edge, which had been especially prepared for rock climbing and abseiling. (This is coming back down using a rope.) I was more than terrified just watching them! I stood with Livvy, watching her sisters each firstly climb up, using fingers and boots to scramble and pull themselves upwards, while attached to a safety line. The higher the girls got, the more terrified I became! Livvy was almost bouncing with excitement in her wheelchair! She was laughing and shaking, rubbing and banging her hands together. One of the instructors saw Livvy in her chair and how excited she was just watching. He said "You know what? She can do this!"

The instructor explained how he could put her in a harness so that she could be pulled up the cliff edge and then lowered down, with the help of a qualified instructor. Well, that's more or less exactly what happened! She had this big safety harness wrapped around her, and she was slowly pulled up the side of the very steep edge to the cliff. She was no longer sitting on the side-lines being a spectator. She was doing it! Life is not a dress rehearsal, and she knew that this was a moment to treasure and enjoy. Livvy was loving every single second of it! She may not have gone up quite as high as the other girls, and she certainly didn't go as fast, but she took part! She was a winner, and I felt desperately proud and happy to see her clasping hands smacking together and her face bursting with pure joy!

At the age of seven, Livvy was used to watching ice skating as her second eldest sister, Eden, used to go for classes regularly at the Silver Blades Ice Skating Rink in Cannock, just a few miles away. Eden had an ice skating birthday, with lots of friends who came along and skated. Livvy, being Livvy, didn't want to be left out, and through clapping clasping hands the signs of excitement started bursting out of her. She wanted to go on the ice with her sister. So, this is exactly what happened! After asking permission, we took her wheelchair onto the ice. Eden and her friends took it in turns to push Livvy in her wheelchair around the little oval shaped ice rink with flashing lights overhead. Livvy absolutely loved it! The faster she was pushed the more she would bounce and laugh and rub her hands with pure joy. She absolutely loved it when her wheelchair was made to spin around on the ice! The girls found it quite hard to push the wheelchair on the ice. This was not only because it was quite heavy, but also because Livvy laughing caused the girls also to be in hysterics! It was so obvious Livvy was loving this so much that it had to become a regular event. We would go when Eden had a lesson, and both she and her friends would also take Livvy out. They each wanted a go pushing Livvy and spinning her around. Livvy quickly learned which people were the quickest and she would do her best to get these people to push her chair! As Eden got better, her lessons needed to move to a bigger ice rink, so we had to go to Coventry. Here, at Planet Ice, Eden was lucky enough to be coached by a young man called David Richardson. He was the UK men's figure skating champion. Of course, Livvy had no problem spotting a handsome young man, and, before you knew it, she also had him taking her around the ice at break neck speed in her wheelchair! She absolutely loved it! The quicker he went and the more fast spins there were, the more excited and happy she was. There are probably not many girls with Rett Syndrome who get taken around on the ice by a national champion, but Livvy can tick that box as done. David would later go on to be a great friend to the family, and a real pleasure to know.

My star of a husband planned a trip to a nearby lake called Chasewater. This is a beautiful bit of water which was about two miles in size around its edge. It had swans, and a lovely café. Sometimes, weather permitting, they'd have canoes at the edge which can be hired for use on the water. Alan got the helmets and life jackets on himself and Livvy. The canoe was the type that you sit on top of rather than inside. He sat on the slightly hollowed out canoe and sat Livvy on his lap. Her face was just full of pure joy! She was splashing the water with her hands and able to hold the paddle. Alan very gently and slowly took her out on the water. Did she love it? Of course she did! The hands were banging together and clasping with total excitement. As expected, when the canoeing came to an end Livvy was soaking wet, and due to all the splashing Alan was also drenched through to the skin! He didn't mind, and seeing her dad so soaked just caused Livvy to laugh even more! These moments are very precious memories I shall always treasure, and nobody can take them away. I think that for

Alan this was a magically precious moment. Livvy taking part in this was huge! It was perhaps something that other parents take for granted. At the time, we knew this was huge and enjoyed every second. Years later, the memories of this day would become, memory gold!

When somebody has any disability, one thing we must never forget, is that while we may have to do things differently, there is one thing which remains constant. Despite whatever communication problems you may have through lack of words, or sight, or speech, a person with a disability always knows when she is having a wonderful time and she always knows when she is having not such a fun time. Livvy certainly knew, and in her own way she could tell us. These laughs and giggles were also moments to cherish for Alan and me.

One day in 2008, we were visited by a representative from a firm called Tomcat. These people design and build trikes for children and adults who have visual, spatial, physical or neurological difficulties. The chap brought a trike and thought that Livvy might like to have a go on it. I remember explaining that Livvy wouldn't have the strength in her legs to be able to ride a trike. Despite my thoughts, Livvy was shown the three-wheeler and placed on the seat which was designed to support her. The next thing I remember was chasing her up the street, as she was off! Livvy absolutely loved this and I knew immediately she had to have it! That was not as easy to do as it was to say! These trikes came in at about £800, and that was far beyond our budget! Thanks to my wonderful family and friends, and their tireless efforts in fundraising, we were soon able to get Livvy her own pink trike. She absolutely loved it! Livvy was on this as much as she could be. My other girls had all enjoyed having bikes, so in my view it was awesome that Livvy could also share this experience.

Livvy always had an eye for a handsome young chap, and, when the European Soccer Championships came on television in 2008, she had a fully blown love of football! I could never afford to take her to a game, and at the time, I didn't know how she would cope with a crowd. In hindsight, I think she would have coped just fine. Livvy loved watching England play. I am not sure if she knew or cared if England were winning or losing, but she found it extremely exciting and loved it when Mum shouted at the television! The European Championship Finals were hosted by Austria and Switzerland, and it was during these finals that she started to have an obsession for Steven Gerrard! Every time Steven Gerrard came on television to talk about the build up to a game, or talk about the team performance after a game, Livvy would go crazy at the television! I personally found it a little disappointing, being a Manchester United fan that Livvy's big football crush would be on a Liverpool player! Hearing his name, or seeing him on the screen, would send Livvy all doddery and giddy!

One day I took Livvy shopping with me and I met Alan's mother, Brenda, at a local shopping centre. Brenda was a wonderful nan to all the girls, but Livvy had her wrapped around her little finger! As we walked past a sports store in the shopping centre Livvy wasted no time in spotting the white England football shirts! She started looking at me, and pointing and creating in a way only a child without words can! She so wanted that shirt! I looked at the price and it was a ridiculous price for a shirt.

I said, "No way mate, you can't have that so you'll have to do without this time." Livvy was not ready to give up yet. She looked Brenda right in the eye and then looked at the shirt and then back at her and as clear as a bell she said "Nan." It was years since we had heard Livvy speak and this was not only clear, but in context, communicating her wishes. Just because she had Rett didn't mean that Livvy didn't know what she wanted, but she would be so frustrated, unable to tell us, on most occasions. Brenda and I just burst into tears and cried, unable to believe that we had just heard Livvy speak for the first time in years! I can only imagine what other people watching made of our sudden outburst of tears! As you can imagine, after that, of course she had to have the shirt! Livvy was delighted. Inside the shop, the assistant found one of the correct size and turned it around asking if we would like a name on the back. I said, "No it's just fine as it is." Livvy understood this conversation perfectly well, and it was anything but fine! She immediately started to kick off again. The understanding was very much still there, and by combination of facial expressions, shaking and loud noises, she made it clear to us that this shirt needed to have a number 4 and Gerrard across the back. This now was one very happy girl! Livvy totally loved this shirt, and, when she had it on, Livvy thought she looked the bee's knees! It may have been expensive to buy when on benefits, but if you could have seen how much happiness it brought to her, then you would have agreed, it was money well spent. Getting the shirt washed was a nightmare, as she hated not having it on. Later we had to buy her a second England shirt in order that we could put one in the washing machine. I have to confess, I picked a red one as the second shirt and accidently forgot to put the name of her favourite Liverpool and England player across the back! The white England shirt Brenda bought for Livvy was such a treasured possession, and so precious. Years later I still treasure that white shirt, and the fabulous memory of the day when she got it, and the joy on her face each time she wore it! That was a good year for Livvy, packed with so many good memories. She and Rachel were together every day, in every lesson and always played together. In the summer, we would also get together outside school and go up to SNAP. This stood for Special Needs Adventure Playground, which Livvy loved. It was only a short distance away in Cannock. Livvy used to love playing out in the garden there, and when she couldn't walk she would lie on the swings in the specially adapted playground. It had a softball room and it had a sensory room. We could go here on any day and it was a good place for just relaxing. Some of it was outside with a climbing frame, a zip wire and more. It was perfect for us, because I could take all four girls and they could play together. There was also a trampoline. There were few places they could all play together. I would meet up with

Rachel's mum here, and we became great friends. I could never thank Sue enough for the phone call she'd made which had caused Livvy to be transferred, and ultimately saved, by Birmingham Children's Hospital, in her darkest hour!

Despite so many good things going on in Livvy's life in 2008, she still had the urge to pick up and eat anything she could! One evening the girls were all in the dining room and Kennedy had placed her homework on the desk which was next to the table. I called the girls to sit at the table as our evening meal was ready. Kennedy went to sit at the far end so she was stuck in her place by the table. Livvy was still crawling around on the floor at this point, because Alan hadn't placed her in her special chair. Suddenly Livvy reached up and grabbed a huge chunk from the corner of Kennedy's homework! This was a lengthy bit of homework. It was for Design, and Kennedy had been tasked to design an electronic light. She had done this in great detail and coloured it in beautifully. I still remember clearly, the horror on Kennedy's face, at the age of twelve, when Livvy finished off eating her homework! We couldn't help much through fits of laughter, and Kennedy couldn't get out to stop it due to the table. This wasn't just an evening's homework or something which could be printed again. It had taken weeks! While everyone laughed, Kennedy was scared, because the deadline for handing this in was the next day. The destruction was total! I remember Kennedy and I both laughing almost to tears as I wrote that most unbelievable of letters to the school. "Sorry, my daughter Kennedy is not able to bring her homework in today, because her sister has eaten it…" It was so funny! The teacher didn't believe Kennedy and told her that nobody's sister eats their homework. She just told him "You haven't met Livvy!"

Grabbing things was Livvy's speciality, and all the girls had long hair. When in a mischievous mood, she would love grabbing the hair of her sister Kennedy or Eden. They would often go in for a hug and Livvy would clamp on to big clumps of hair. She didn't pull it out. She however kept hold and you were not going anywhere! I remember one of many times she held on. Kennedy or Eden would be yelling "Guys please help me!" Nobody did! They all just laughed and this would make Livvy laugh even more!

Kennedy was a talented singer and loved singing in school concerts. Her number one fan would be Livvy. Livvy loved to hear her sister singing, 'Somewhere Over the Rainbow' from the film 'The Wizard of Oz'. When Kennedy sang in the school concert at Shire Oak School, we took Livvy. She was clapping, bouncing in her seat and shrieking with total pleasure and excitement seeing her sister dressed up and singing to everybody.

We still had to be careful with food all the time. If you left your meal, it was always important to check you'd left it out of Livvy's reach. In her mind, once she had finished her food, then yours would be fair game and she would go for it. We went to Pizza Hut one day for a rare treat, and, once we had all taken our coats off and been seated, I noticed Livvy was tucking into some garlic bread. She had somehow managed to help herself to food on the next table. I gave them the well-practiced apology, and, luckily, they didn't mind! There are many understanding people in this world, and, thankfully, Livvy had a habit, on most occasions, of just stealing food from people who understood!

If I took Livvy to the Supermarket, I would put her in the seat in the trolley. Turning my back on her for a second would come at a price! Each time I got to the check out and paid, the cheese or bread or anything she could reach would have a large bite taken out of it!

There wasn't any limit to the things she would bite! One day, Alan and I were waiting at Birmingham Children's Hospital, when he put his finger near her mouth. It was at this point Alan knew he had messed up! She bit it, and bit it hard! Once he had extracted his painful finger I remember Livvy being amused by her actions and Alan was walking up and down holding his hand, trying his hardest not to cry! All I could say was "Alan, why did you put your finger in her mouth?" We would laugh about it on every following visit to the hospital. Livvy had more than once taken a bite out of Alan! She would go to him and move in to have a cuddle and, just when he wasn't expecting it, she would bite his shoulder! To Livvy this was being affectionate, and she would be laughing as she tried to take chunks out of Alan. When you have a daughter with Rett, you must learn to laugh at a lot at things others might not find so funny! I am so grateful for this year when so many good things happened.

When I had been in hospital earlier, at the time Livvy had been so very ill, I'd met a couple called Ann-Marie and Paul, who were at the hospital with their son Ryan, who was also disabled. So many people along my journey with Livvy became friends and helped, but Ann-Marie and Paul deserve a special mention, because they basically changed my whole thoughts on disability and taught me how to live with it. Livvy had been put in the same bay as young Ryan, who had Cerebral Palsy' and also a movement disorder. This turned out to be one of the best things which could have happened to Livvy. Ryan was a couple of years older than Livvy and went to the same school. While Rachel may have been Livvy's best friend, Ryan would be classed as a boyfriend to her. They would always be giggling and trying to be near each other. This friendship was one which would last.

Anne-Marie helped me with so much and told me so many things I didn't know about looking after a disabled child. I was still paying for nappies, not knowing I could get these for free. And I didn't know we could get the assistance of an occupational therapist. She told us how we could get a special chair to put her in while she was having a seizure, to keep her safe. Prior to meeting Anne-Marie I knew nothing and didn't really have a clue what I might be entitled to. Alan and I bonded with them and we became great friends. While we bonded, Livvy and Ryan became inseparable. Anne-Marie talked about going camping and in disbelief I said, "You can't go camping with a wheelchair."

"Yes, you can," she answered. She gave us a tent, and all the stuff we needed, and off we went camping. We went to Barmouth, in North Wales, and had a glorious week. We had so much fun it was crazy! We nearly killed Livvy's wheelchair because she kept going in the sea with it! We got rust and all sorts on it, but this really didn't matter, because Livvy was having fun! Fun is what matters, and fun had been in such precious short supply for Livvy, prior to this year, and she had some catching up to do. Livvy so loved the sea, and also the tent! It was eye opening for us to realise we could go camping. On another occasion, we all went camping together, along with Ryan and his parents, to Anglesey. This was another brilliant and magic trip, despite Livvy and Ryan almost getting both our families thrown off the site! It was advertised as a site which catered for, and welcomed people with, disabilities. We arrived and found that they had a portable toilet outside on ground level, and' as far as being equipped for disabled people, that was the extent of it. We had made a long journey and thought "Fine, let's just get on with it.'' We put the two-family tents up next to each other, and did the whole sitting around the fire thing. We were just two families enjoying each other's company. When it came to bedtime, the kids were sent to bed, and I told Livvy to go to sleep. She found the whole situation hilarious! She couldn't believe she was sleeping in a tent, with her boyfriend in a tent a few metres away! We had to tell Livvy to be quiet, because she was laughing so much! Ryan heard this and, of course, started laughing also! Then he was told to be quiet also, which caused Livvy to laugh. The whole cycle continued for some time and got louder and louder! There was a rule on this campsite, no noise after 11pm. Somebody must have complained about the kids, because the next morning one of the campsite staff came to speak about the noise. In a stern voice, he said "One of your children was causing trouble last night laughing. Now which one was it?" We pointed to Livvy and Ryan sitting in their wheelchairs. The poor fella looked at these two and he just didn't know what to say. I explained "We did try to tell them to go to sleep, but they thought it was hilarious and wouldn't!" They had just giggled and laughed all night. When these two were together they were trouble! They couldn't help but laugh and be happy in each other's company!

At New Year, we all went to Anne-Marie's house to celebrate as two families together. Paul had Livvy up doing the chocolate fountain which she absolutely loved. I noticed that Ryan was laughing hysterically, even more than normal. I couldn't understand why. Had I missed something? "Why are you laughing?" I asked him. Of course, he didn't answer, but while I had been trying to find out what was funny, Livvy had left the chocolate fountain and crawled around the back of me, and Ryan could see that she was sitting drinking my wine!

Our friendship and enjoyment of camping caused me to join a charity called Special Kids in UK. This was a forum online on which parents all chatted and supported each other, then once a year they would meet up and go camping.

The first time I went it was in Nottingham, and there was one lady called Tia, who I had been so looking forward to meeting after many useful conversations online. Tia was there with her own daughter, who was in a wheelchair eating a biscuit, and Livvy soon caused us to be introduced. Livvy being Livvy managed to get over to her and, of course, grab her biscuit! So, much to my horror, the first conversation I had with Tia, was when I had to make an apology for her daughter's biscuit having been stolen! She understood, but sadly Livvy never stopped there, and her nickname on that camp was 'The Biscuit Thief.' From that point onwards, every time Tia saw Livvy she would get a biscuit ready. She was a little monster when there were biscuits about, and so mischievous it was untrue!

Livvy just loved life! Everything Livvy did, she could turn into an adventure for us all. One-day she would be flirting with the doctors, to the next day becoming 'The Biscuit Thief,' but always with laughter and a smile!

We went also this year to a Parks Resort in Carmarthen, in South Wales. So many memories in this year, but my two main memories of this holiday were, firstly, Livvy ending up with a black eye. Her darling older sister, Kennedy, was supposed to be watching her while I emptied the car, but, instead, she went to choose her bedroom first. While she was doing this, Livvy thought it was a clever idea to do a jumping dive from the sofa and into the bookcase, resulting in a large black eye. Of course, Kennedy had a good telling off, because she was given only one job to do, and had left her sister, who needed watching all the time. Livvy herself was laughing uncontrollably at her sister being in trouble! She was a little mischief sometimes! The second, and far more pleasant, memory from this holiday, was from a day trip we took into Tenby. Tenby is a lovely little seaside town, and we went into one of those cheap seaside jewellery shops. Livvy saw a ring and got very excited looking at it. Many staff and people we meet don't know what to do around Livvy when she is getting all excited, and I expect many parents with a disabled child experience similar. The fella in this shop was very good. He just said, "Would she like to try it on?" Of course, Livvy did try it on, and it fitted perfectly! She instantly fell in love with this ring! We had never bought Livvy any jewellery before, because everything she touched would be placed straight into her mouth. This ring was different. Livvy was so pleased with herself, and thought it looked so smart! We not only spent the rest of the day walking around Tenby with Livvy holding her hand out for everybody to see, but if she got close to anyone she would give them a gentle bash and made sure they turned around and had a good look at her beautiful ring. This was yet another item which became extremely precious to Livvy, which is now still very dear to me today. Livvy could get away with whacking strangers and demanding they look at her ring. This was not all she would get away with!

I loved taking Livvy with me as much as I could but I would always have to ring family and friends before setting off to give them a chance to "Livvy proof" the house. They needed to move anything precious or breakable up high or into another room. I always gave my mum plenty of warning when going to visit with Livvy, and she would check that everything was out of reach. Livvy had a fascination with opening and emptying drawers at my mother's house, and the contents of each drawer would be opened and all over the place as soon as she managed to get into it. My stepdad had a little drawer in which he kept his snacks or sweets to eat when he came home from work. Of course, the day came when Livvy found her Grandad's snack drawer, and, of course, everything was gone very quickly. Of course, as it was Livvy, my dad didn't mind a bit. I don't think he would have reacted in the same way if any of the other girls had done this. That pretty little of face of Livvy's had her Grandad wrapped around her little finger also!

Alan's sister Lorna married David at Shrewsbury Castle, and all four girls, including Livvy, were bridesmaids. Alan and I were panicking, wondering if she would be good. Would she sit through the service? Well, she did sit through the service, sort of, and she loved it! There was one very funny moment in the service when the church was silent and Alan was holding her. She let fly with a huge slap on his cheek. It didn't hurt, but made him jump, and whole church turned and looked to see what was happening. Other than that, she just flapped her bag a bit, which was heard echoing around the hall, but Livvy loved life, and loved this day also. She knew that she looked pretty and that people were looking at her. She didn't enjoy the reception as much, because things were running late, and the food was late, and this caused Livvy to start having a few seizures. It was fortunate that Livvy was good in the service, because I couldn't stay and watch the ceremony. My youngest daughter, who was also a bridesmaid, decided that she did not want to watch the wedding. So I ended up walking around outside with Brodie, instead of watching the wedding. I had taken her outside for some air, and the doors had been locked behind us. Alan was inside with three girls, and I had been stuck outside, walking about with Brodie. There were some American tourists who were outside having come to admire the castle, and Brodie ran up to them and tried to give away her bouquet of bridesmaid flowers!

There were so many memories in this year with Livvy! We all went on a camping holiday in New Quay, in Wales, during the summer. It wasn't exactly camping, but, instead, we rented a large static caravan on a real working farm. The farm had some beautiful cottages which were rented out. We couldn't afford those, so we ended up in the static caravan. The farmer Ian, and his wife, were ever so friendly and kind, and one evening he let Kennedy, Eden and Brodie all have a ride around inside the cab of his tractor. They each loved it! The farmer was aware that Livvy had Rett Syndrome, and said afterwards that it felt wrong that she was missing out. He offered to return with his tractor the following morning, once he had finished lambing, and, one way or another, Livvy would get her ride. He was true to his word, and the very next morning he returned. He pulled from above and we all pushed from below and Livvy was raised up into the cab of the tractor! She sat on his knee looking down on us as the tractor circled the field repeatedly. She was shrieking with joy, and instead of the normal hand clasping and clapping, Livvy was trying to drive the tractor with her hands on the large steering wheel. The big tractor went round and round, and Livvy milked every ounce of fun from each second. I couldn't help noticing that the farmer was also beaming with happiness. He was enjoying the sight of Livvy's total joy, and I knew that he was just another, in the lengthy list of many, whose hearts Livvy had won! He had taken a huge shine to her instantly after meeting. I thought it was so wonderful that he wanted her not to miss out, and he went out of his way to make sure that the ride happened. Life had been hard at times, so when someone made a special effort to do a kind gesture I always appreciated it.

While in the same caravan, Livvy had a day of hysterics, when her younger sister got into trouble. Her sisters being in trouble was always a reason to laugh! Brodie was refusing to put some rubbish in the bin and Alan shouted at her "Brodie, put the rubbish in the bin." Livvy just started laughing and laughing. For the remainder of that day, each time any of us said "Brodie, put the rubbish in the bin," Livvy would be creased up in laughter. What a funny child! Despite what life had chucked at her, what a happy child!

The highs and lows of this year would not be complete without mentioning the visits for physiotherapy at the Donkey Sanctuary in Sutton Coldfield. What a fantastic place! They did so much for special needs kids who not only got up close and personal with the donkeys, but could ride them also. A young lady called Amber, whose mother ran the sanctuary, took a special liking to Livvy, and she took a shine to her. Amber, while being young and pretty wore her hair in a bob style. She was very old school around the kids. She would tell Livvy to straighten her back and Livvy would shoot a dirty look back at her. She was trying her best. Livvy loved Amber to pieces and each time we went, she'd be looking out for her. If Amber wasn't there, Livvy would be far from happy. The physio here was exceptional, and gave us hope of miracles. It was here that Livvy took a few steps once, independently. I was sitting holding an excited Livvy against my lap as she looked at the donkeys, desperate to be near them. Off she walked by herself, without me. In her mind, Livvy turned, and her face said, "I'm not waiting for you Mum, I want to see them now." This was a surreal moment in a place filled with inspirational people, and maybe deserves a book by itself. For this reason, the sanctuary, the donkeys and the staff were added to the list of places and people very special to our hearts.

Chapter 6

Alan had taken advantage of everyone being in bed, and used the peace and quiet to stay up until 1.30 am on the morning of 7th November 2008. He shouldn't have done because he knew that he, Eden and I were getting up ridiculously early that day, as we were taking Eden to compete in an Ice Skating competition. Just before going to bed, Alan had quietly sneaked into Livvy's room to check on her. She was awake and had seen her Dad come in. Alan put his hand on her head and looked down as he said, "Goodnight Treacle." It was just a normal everyday thing. A simple pleasure making sure your child is ok. Little did he know, while lovingly saying those immortal words, that this would be the last time he would see his daughter alive!

The alarm clock sounded at 3.30 am, which is a crazy time to be getting up. There were lots of things we needed to get ready prior to leaving for the ice skating competition. We decided not to wake Eden straight away, as she could travel in her pyjamas. I quickly got myself washed and dressed because I knew that Diane, my mum, was going to be here soon with my stepfather, Trevor. They had volunteered to look after Kennedy, Brodie and Livvy for the day while we took Eden to her competition.

I went downstairs once ready, just as Diane and Trevor were arriving. I know I should never have gone into Livvy's room and risked waking her. Once Livvy is awake, she is awake, and I knew I was doing nobody any favours at that time in the morning! Diane said "Just leave her Sara, we'll

85

watch her. She will be fine." I couldn't. There was no way I could travel without a quick peep to see that she was ok. Very quietly I sneaked in. Livvy was motionless. Girls with Rett are almost always moving or fidgeting. Even when sleeping they move a bit. She wasn't moving even a tiny bit. She was unresponsive. I thought, at first, that she was in one of her really deep sleeps. I opened the bedroom door fully allowing the light from the house to spill across the room, so I could see better. I called for Alan, asking him to come and take a look. I felt numb with fear, which was almost making it difficult to breathe. "Alan, can you check Livvy? I'm not sure she is breathing," I said as he came to the room. He assured me I was being my usual overprotective and paranoid self and I needed to pull myself together. He quickly checked her and looked at me and back at Livvy. She was warm, she was very warm, and in words I can't remember Alan confirmed she was not breathing.

If we had been on a plane at this time, the feeling inside would have been that we had just lost cabin pressure and fast. A panic and crippling chaos consumed my thoughts, and everything around became background noise while my head struggled with the reality of what was happening and tried to find time to panic. Alan was calmer, and immediately made a call to the emergency services, requesting an urgent ambulance. Diane and Trevor must have heard what was happening, and my stepfather rushed to Livvy and worked frantically on the bed having dropped the cot sides on the bed so that he could start attempting to resuscitate his granddaughter. Brodie and Eden were still asleep, completely unaware of what was occurring while they slept. I was screaming inside with fear and panic, and also completely unaware that my eldest daughter, Kennedy, was stirring from her sleep and about to get up due to the noise.

Alan went down to meet the paramedic, who arrived extremely quickly at our front door. He ran to the bedroom and took over from Trevor, who had been attempting to resuscitate Livvy. There was little conversation other than that Alan had been asked to go and look out for the ambulance which would be following. He waited downstairs while I stood paralyzed by a mother's worst nightmare unfolding before my eyes. There was a brief radio communication, and suddenly the paramedic scooped up Livvy and ran through the house, almost knocking Alan over as he carried her with the speed and determination of a rugby player running with the ball, straight into the back of the ambulance. The ambulance team and paramedic didn't waste a single second! Only one person could travel with Livvy to the hospital, and Alan was both calmer and closer. There was also no time for debating who would go. Alan said later that he couldn't do much to help and if anything, he got the impression that they didn't want him in there, as they wanted to get stuck in 100 % attempting to save our daughter's life. I was still in my daughter's bedroom with Diane and Trevor, thinking I might be able to go with Livvy also, but, in a confused panic, I was just trying to grab some shoes. I remember not being able to find any shoes. There were probably several pairs, but, in the confusion, I just couldn't find anything. Eventually I had footwear, and Trevor said he would whiz me over to the hospital. Diane stayed at the house to look after Kennedy, Eden and Brodie. Only Kennedy had woken, and she had been a silent witness to all this noise and frantic panic. The journey to the Walsall Manor Hospital was a straight forward one normally, but on this occasion, Trevor made a couple of detours to try and beat the traffic and arrive as quickly as possible. These didn't work, and the drive to the hospital felt like an eternity for both me and also Alan who was nervously waiting. We had very quickly been asked to go into a private waiting room. It was a suffocating little room, with no windows and just a few chairs. The hollow acoustics caused by the bare walls felt cold, as the ticking clock reminded me just how precious every second of life really is. Neither of us really knew what to say. I still have no idea how long we both waited nervously, holding hands in this room while doctors were working on our precious girl. It felt like an hour, but could have been much less. The door kept opening. At first it was Trevor, who joined us having managed to park the car, and then my father Phil arrived. He was followed by Alan's mum, Brenda. Each was concerned and asking questions I could hardly find the breath to answer! Each time the door opened, all I desperately wanted was someone who was going to tell me she was ok. Each person who walked in must have only seen a disappointed or despairing look on my face. Alan had not been on good terms with his stepfather, Anthony, and even he turned up at the hospital. He didn't come in but rang from outside. Anthony had been Brenda's partner prior to Chris and had raised Alan since he was a young boy. It wasn't the ideal time for a family catch up. The minutes passed slowly and awkwardly. We waited. Then we waited some more.

The door finally opened and a young looking Asian female doctor entered our tiny waiting room. She was slight in build and wore a clean white overcoat over her own clothing. Her serious eyes gave me the news before her mouth even opened. She took a deep breath and then said "Mr and Mrs Meredith, we have worked extremely hard to do all we can for Livvy, but I'm sorry to say, that we couldn't get her to start breathing again."

This young doctor was clearly deeply upset, and her face and voice were so kind and sympathetic. How could such a lovely person be giving such dreadful news? Other words were said after this, but I will never remember these! At this point I was broken! My soul felt as if it had been torn out and stamped on! Everything was background noise, and I found my chest tightening, and I could barely breathe due to the torture of coming to terms with this news!

I was suffocating, unable to cry, and had to leave the room and go outside with Alan for fresh air. It took a while to pull ourselves together, and, once I could breathe, all I wanted was to see my baby girl. I didn't think things could get any worse, but I was wrong.

We were not allowed at this time to see Livvy. We certainly couldn't be on our own with her. The cause of her death was now immediately to become an investigation, so, still, we had to remain distant observers. We knew where she was. She was in a resuscitation room split into four sections. She was in a far corner. A mother should never see screens being placed around her child. These screens are to protect other staff or the public from having the shock of seeing a child who was dead. These screens prevented Alan and I seeing our child on her way for all over body x-rays, which were a starting point to the investigation as to why she had suddenly died. I've never experienced a more harrowing and helpless moment in my life, as staff attempted to shield Livvy from our sight, as they whisked her away!

I used this time to ring my mum, Diane, who was sitting at home looking after Kennedy, Eden and Brodie. I wanted to tell Livvy's sisters myself, but I couldn't relay anything. I was frozen, and words wouldn't come out. I was unaware that, when Diane answered the phone, Kennedy was sitting watching her. The look on Diane's face told Kennedy the dreadful news without my mum having to say a word. It was a call she had been frantic to receive, but when I made it, there was nothing but a crippling silence. Firstly, I couldn't find the words, and, due to shock and the tightening of my chest, I just couldn't talk. The pause seemed endless until I could find the strength to mutter "Mum, she's gone." I don't remember anything else being said, and I just passed the phone to my stepdad, Trevor.

Eden had been oblivious to most of what happened this morning, as she had been left sleeping during the earlier chaos. It was for Eden's competition we were getting up, but we hadn't planned on waking her until she needed to get in the car. Kennedy had woken Eden to let her know. This is not a task any sister ever wants to do.

We waited and waited while the staff did x-rays and any other tests they needed to do. After an endless wait, Livvy was returned to the resuscitation room once more. She remained hidden behind the screens. It was now that Alan and I were told we could come and see Livvy. I nervously went behind the screens. There lay my beautiful girl! We were finally allowed to sit with her for a while. The nurse said, "You can have as long you want." They didn't think what they were saying, because you can't stay there forever can you? No parent will want to walk out of a room in these circumstances. It's an admission of what happened. I never wanted to leave. How could they say, "You can stay as long as you want," when clearly you can't? I didn't want to leave, but I also knew the other girls were at home and they would be hysterical by now. Those words were making me angry. It is a load of crap, because you can't just stay there forever. You have to move at some point. I didn't know what to do. I didn't know what was that point.

Livvy looked so peaceful and happy! They had brushed her hair before we came in. In a crazy way, Livvy had never looked so beautiful! My faith is very strong, but at this moment, as I saw her lying in pyjamas, my faith was tested. Rett Syndrome robs girls of their peace, and they are never still. They are constantly fidgeting and moving. Even

91

when she was sleeping Livvy would be moving about most of the time. Now she looked different. She didn't look traumatized or upset, just smiling with a beautiful smile. I am so thankful for that. It was if she was smiling and saying "Goodbye Mum, I'm going home. See you soon!" This was all I had to hold on to!

We'd hugged her when we first came in. I didn't want to leave. I felt I had failed her. I should have known something was wrong, I could have gone into the room a bit sooner, but I didn't.

Staff had taken Livvy's footprints, and also a bit of her hair to give me. It was a nice gesture, but I wasn't up to a conversation about that. Brenda took these and looked after them for me. I felt that taking these at this moment was acknowledging she had gone, and I wasn't ready for that. I just wanted someone to come and tell me it had been a mistake.

I don't remember how long I stayed. It was a long time. I think it was less than three hours. I never wanted to leave. As time passed, I noticed the hospital was getting louder and louder. Normal everyday activity was continuing just the other side of these screens, and I almost felt as if I was an inconvenience. "Stay as long as you need," kept going through my mind. I held Livvy again and saw changes. Her colour was a little pale, and the warm skin I remembered when I touched her in the bedroom was now icy cold. She was totally cold. It was just starting to sink in, as her cooling made me feel her soul had now left her body and she was at peace in a better place. The time was coming, and I wrestled with two emotions. Part of me hoped that the noise in the hospital might wake her up, while in reality I knew that when I left her, I would be leaving her forever! I was never going to get her back! I got up to leave, battling with these two emotions, and can only remember falling to the floor, begging the nurses to help. Nothing was real! I was not ready! I sat longer, and saw the changes and the warmth leave. I started to think about my other girls, Kennedy, Eden and Brodie worrying at home. It was now I decided the time was right. If Livvy had been able to talk, then she would have been telling me to go home and see her sisters. After we'd both given her a slow, cold, last kiss, we quietly left her, to rest in peace.

Without my knowledge, while Alan and I had been sitting saying goodbye to our inspirational little angel, Livvy, the police had arrived at our home where Diane was waiting, looking after the three girls. The police went in and took lots of photographs and took Livvy's medicines. Some things were moved, and Diane took the girls to her house. Nobody was allowed in the house until the senior investigating officer, a Detective Chief Inspector, had arrived. Alan and I were given a lift home in the back of a police car, driven by this senior officer. My head was not in a good place, and nearly everything anyone said to me became only background noise. I was really struggling to process anything new after the emotional carnage my brain was trying to process. I do remember the look on Alan's face as we turned the corner and he saw two police officers in their bright fluorescent jackets standing waiting at our front door, like a pair of guards at Buckingham Palace! This felt so surreal! This sort of thing happens to other people. We were both aware that the neighbours would be looking out. Curtains would be twitching. While barely conscious of this, neither Alan or I could care less. Our daughter had just died. We really didn't care about anything. These moments were morbidly dark. The depth of despair was impossible for either of us to measure. Alan and I exchanged fewer words than you would imagine as this morning continued. One thing I do remember very strongly is that neither Alan nor I wanted to be there anymore. We wanted to be with Livvy. Everything that happened in front of us didn't matter. Nothing mattered. I am not saying we were planning on jumping off the nearest bridge, but we didn't want to be in this world any longer. Alan had his pain, and it was severe. He also felt the agony I was in. If I was in agony, he was also suffering. My faith had been little comfort to either of us on the day Livvy passed. The wonderful staff at the hospital had not managed to spare us this. There were only three reasons we remained in this world and without these reasons, Alan and I would have found a way to be with Livvy. These reasons had names, Kennedy, Eden and Brodie. They hadn't left our thoughts, and, at the same time as we were absorbing this juggernaut of grief, I was also trying to work out how we were going to support and help our other wonderful daughters. They also had to cope with their grief.

Inside the house, police were still filming and photographing, and Doctor Drew, who we knew well, was also there to observe. Livvy's room had been downstairs, so we really couldn't avoid being aware of all that was going on. I then saw Livvy's toy, Noddy. It made me so angry. I couldn't say why I was angry, but I think Noddy got blamed! I'm not sure if I was furious that Livvy was at the hospital without her beloved Noddy or was I furious that he was here and she wasn't? I was angry I couldn't bring her home. I was angry I couldn't save her. I am a mum, I should have known, I should have been able to do something. I had failed her. I was angry, and seeing Noddy reminded me of this and made me feel I'd let her down!

I didn't mind the police being in the house searching, seizing, photographing and videoing whatever they wanted. We had nothing to hide. The house felt busy and alive. It felt as if we were part of a process, and I hoped we might get some answers. Eventually, they decided their enquiries were complete, and it was time for them to leave. As we shut the door behind the officers, the emptiness struck once more. Nobody does this. What am I supposed to do now?

When any parent loses a child, it is terrible! If your daughter has Rett Syndrome, there is a difference. As they grow older, children with Rett Syndrome can become more dependent on you, rather than less. They still have nappies which need changing, they will grab anything they can and either break it or try and swallow it. They have no fear, so a constant vigilant eye is needed for every second to ensure they don't hurt themselves. It is more than a full-time job, it is 24/7. Now what shall I do? I can't just sit. I have never had those few moments of doing nothing. Having Livvy required constant attention and focus from either Alan or me. Suddenly, this had been taken away, and there was a vacuum to fill. We had been so used to having every second filled. Nine years of caring for someone! Suddenly before the sun had even gone down I realised just how much we used to do for her! This emptiness would later almost drive me insane! Later, I would end up ironing knickers and tea towels and doing anything I could to fill the time. I just didn't know what I was supposed to do with this extra time!

There was still one more painful task we needed to complete on this first evening back at the house. We needed to talk to Kennedy, Eden and Brodie about what had happened. They had to leave the house when the police had turned up to film and seize Livvy's medication. They were at Diane's house and it was she who fetched them back later this same day. Having previously frozen on the phone, I wasn't sure what I was going to say. Speaking was so difficult! I remember all three girls running in and just hugging us both. We just hugged and hugged as a family. I don't recollect if any of us said anything. I knew that they knew, and we just hugged them and they hugged each other.

Each daughter found a little comfort by taking one of Livvy's favourite toys. Brodie, the youngest, took Leo the Lion, which still has pride of place on her bed to this day. Eden had the Rett Syndrome Toy which had been created in America. This had been made especially for little girls with

Rett and sent over by a friend in America. Eden called it Kitty Cat and it was a pink spotted kitten. Kennedy, the eldest, took Noddy. All the girls still have these treasured items. Kennedy took Noddy with her when studying at University.

In the days following Livvy's passing, there had to be an in-depth investigation into how and why she'd died. This had to involve a pathologist from Birmingham Children's Hospital. It was realized early on that Livvy hadn't died due to a seizure or a heart irregularity. She therefore had to have a very detailed investigation to establish the cause. The investigation, and subsequent tests, took a long time, and, because of this Livvy wasn't laid to rest until December. Following all these tests, Livvy was eventually returned to the Co-op Funeral Home in Brownhills, which was only a stone's throw from Chasewater Lake, upon which she'd enjoyed such a fantastic day drenching her father on a canoe! The Co-op staff were also extremely kind to us and set a date for the funeral, which was to take place at Streetly Crematorium, on 3rd December 2008.

Livvy had a favourite dress, which was long, pink and covered with flowers. It was a summer dress and didn't have sleeves. She'd fallen in love with this dress in Matalan and grabbed it, refusing to let go. Every time she put it on her face would light up. She was always flashing her knickers in it, but that was just Livvy! I was concerned, as a month had passed since Livvy had gone, and she'd changed a lot in this time. She couldn't just wear a dress without sleeves, and I was very concerned about how she looked. This was very important to me. So off I went shopping for a new cardigan. Some people thought I was crazy going out to buy a brand-new cardigan to put on a dead child. I thought it was the most normal thing in the world. No mother wants to know her daughter doesn't look her best. I visited many shops before I saw one which was perfect in Adams in Walsall. I loved it as soon as I saw it, but they didn't have one in Livvy's size. Alan's mum jumped straight on the train and went all the way into Birmingham and bought one from the Adams shop there. I wanted things to be just right for Livvy, and bless you, Brenda, doing this for me. The cardigan was a beautiful mixture of different pinks with a little hood. It just matched perfectly with Livvy's favourite dress. We knew it cost a lot, and we knew where it was going. It didn't matter. This was the last time we would pick her clothes and she was going to look perfect!

She did look beautiful in her outfit when we went to see her in the funeral home. It was weird going to see Livvy in the funeral home. It was her, but it didn't look like her! She'd been passed for a month and she had changed so much! It almost wasn't my Livvy! They had put makeup on her, lots of makeup. She was nine years old and at that age they don't wear makeup, but obviously she had to. I'll always remember she had lipstick on and it was too much! I just wiped it off her. We had chosen her toy, Tinkerbell, to go with her. Livvy always had to have her fingers wrapped up in Tinkerbell's hair, so it was only right she should have her company here. The girls didn't come and see Livvy at the funeral home. I didn't let them come, and I'm so glad I didn't. I wanted them to remember Livvy how she was when she was alive. As she lay here was not the way Livvy would want to be remembered. The girls were too young, and they had their memories of Livvy, and that's what I wanted them to hold on to. If she had looked as she did at the hospital, I might have allowed them to see her, but now she didn't look like Livvy. Her school teachers came and said she looked beautiful and peaceful. I agreed, but she just looked very different! She looked so much smaller also! When we'd left her at the hospital, she was cold, but she didn't look cold. As she lay resting in the funeral parlour, she not only felt cold, but looked very cold also. This coldness reinforced that it just wasn't Livvy lying here anymore. It was merely her physical being, and, as far as I was concerned, her soul was dancing with Jesus at this point. That was the thought I had to keep holding onto. There is a part of me that wishes I hadn't gone back to see Livvy looking like this. The funeral home staff were so nice and understanding, and, as we left, they informed me that the parlour was open until 8 o'clock that night. We were welcome to visit Livvy again. I didn't go back. I knew my departure at mid-afternoon was to be my last time seeing Livvy. The more I saw Livvy in that coffin, a month after she had died, the more I thought about it and it was not good. I still don't know if the decision not to return with the girls was the right one, but, at the time, this felt the only sensible decision. I thought we should all remember Livvy as being full of life. Even if your head can comprehend it, the experience of seeing a dead person leaves you with an imprint you don't need. She was my daughter and I had to go, but I didn't think the girls were ready for this. I'd gone along with the expectation of being able to hug her and breathe in all those last memories, but it wasn't her! The expectation and the reality were very different. My Grandparents visited and said their goodbyes, as did several of her teachers. The funeral had been arranged in school time, so not all the teachers who wanted to come were able to. The ones who couldn't visited her at the parlour instead.

You would have thought that things couldn't get much harder, but the sad reality was things did. Alan's stepfather, who had separated from Brenda years earlier, had turned up at the hospital on the day Livvy died. He had shown brief moments of being the distraught grandparent, but when Alan informed him that the date of the funeral had been set, his stepfather, Anthony, said that he might not be able to make it. Alan told him "This is your granddaughter's funeral. What are you doing?" Anthony's new girlfriend had planned a couple of days away in Scotland, and wasn't letting anything change these plans! Alan and I both thought, when we asked him to see what he could sort out, that they would reschedule and we'd see him there to say his goodbyes. But he did finally call and confirm that he wouldn't be attending. Alan was understandably in a rage! How could anything be more important than attending your granddaughter's funeral? Alan told Anthony that he was washing his hands of him, and wanted no further relationship with him. Anthony treated the whole occasion with such indifference that Alan became angrier than I'd ever known him in my whole life! When Anthony phoned the funeral parlour trying to arrange a delivery of flowers for Livvy, it made things even worse. His evil new girlfriend had been on the phone to our house, screaming abuse, while we attempted to come to terms with our grief. Now he had the audacity to assume he could just send some flowers! Anthony was not allowed to send his flowers. He was impolitely informed exactly where he could shove his flowers! Anthony's failure to be there when it mattered cost him the relationship with the boy he had raised as his own son. Similar behaviour would later also lose him a relationship with the girl he'd raised as a daughter, but that's another story.

I put a great deal of time and thought into the planning of Livvy's funeral. I almost became obsessed, not surprisingly, as this was the last thing I would be able to do for her. I chose the flowers, and everyone had to have a yellow rose, because this was our family flower. Alan had bought me yellow roses after our first daughter was born, and it became a tradition with each daughter that followed. As Livvy had enjoyed yellow roses in life, it felt only right we should have yellow roses here also. Great thought had also gone into deciding upon which music we would play. We picked one of her favourites, the Tinkerbell Song, as Livvy just looked like Tinkerbell.

We'd been great supporters and friends of our local donkey sanctuary, where they did so much to help children with special needs. Livvy had enjoyed some of her happiest moments here. When I rang Amber, who'd looked after Livvy here, she was also very upset by our news. Livvy and Amber had enjoyed a brilliant chemistry between them, and Livvy never wanted anybody else to take her on rides when she went riding. It was a kind of love/ hate relationship! I recalled Livvy's eyes lighting up when she saw Amber and those dirty looks when told to straighten her back!

Amber asked if it would be ok to bring Livvy's favourite donkey, Alvis, to the funeral. I thought this would be so special, but had no idea just how special it would be! We had just one black car for immediate family, and others followed in their own cars behind. When we turned up, this brown and grey donkey was waiting to greet Livvy. After the funeral, Alvis was renamed "Alvis Livvy, " which was the sweetest thing they could have done!

At funerals it is common to ask for donations instead of flowers, and we did this also. It surprised a few when I asked for the donations to go to the donkey sanctuary instead of Rett Syndrome, but at this time I was so angry with Rett Syndrome for taking my child away that I couldn't even think about acknowledging it! It took me a very long time before I was ready to even think of talking about Rett Syndrome. The presence of the donkey made the funeral a beautiful occasion! In hindsight, there were other things I would also like to have done, but we don't get warning and practice, luckily, at having to organise funerals for our children, so I had to be content with what we'd managed. The service had to be a celebration of her life. Everybody patted Alvis as they went in and he waited outside so that everybody could pat him as they left the service. I'd brought nine silver star shaped balloons for the children present to release after the service. When they came out they all gathered together to release the balloons. As they gathered and released these, there was total silence. Even the wind fell silent as the children released the balloons. Alvis chose that exact second to do one almighty poop! A sombre moment suddenly turned so hilarious! The people looking after the donkey were embarrassed and apologetic, but it was perfect! It was precisely what Livvy would have wanted! The laughter was belly-busting, and so typical of living with Livvy. The kids giggled first, which gave the adults the freedom to laugh out loud. It was so typical, and I swear that, if she could have tickled that donkey into pooping at that moment, she would have done! The whole moment when balloons were to be released was very poignant and hard, but it was engulfed in a laughter which was so special, and so Livvy!

A dear friend, and talented poet, also wrote the words below, to be spoken during the highly emotional service which were so comforting on a very difficult day.

Kendra's Poem

In May 1999 a little star fell from the sky.

Little did we know back then, how deeply you would touch our lives,

With your wild blonde hair and cheeky grin,

With that special sparkle in your eyes.

You touched every heart that met you,

With that dazzling wonderful smile.

Your determination to succeed and win,

Made us forget our own problems for a while.

For seeing such a will so strong,

In someone so very small,

Gave us hope and inspiration,

That in Life you, must give your all.

Whether it was watching on Cbeebie's Fireman Sam,

Or Giggling to Lazy Town,

The simple things in life, you loved,

And appreciated your world that was around.

And though your mummy and daddy will miss you,

As will your sisters, friends and family too.

Some stars need to return home before us,

And this is what happened to you.

Because sometimes those little stars,

That on earth to us shine so bright,

Need to return to their beautiful sky once more,

And keep watch over the ones they love at night.

Every time we look up at that big old sky,

And wonder how you are,

We will see one of the stars twinkle brightly,

And know you are smiling at us from afar.

And so, to you Livvy our precious angel,

Full of life, of hope and of light,

So until we meet again, to you Livvy we wish you the sweetest dreams

And for now our darling... Goodnight

The celebration of Livvy's life continued with a gathering of friends and family at the Anchor Inn at Brownhills straight after the funeral, at about one o'clock. It was a nice gathering, with everyone sharing their memories. I was just in busy mode. A few of Livvy's friends, teachers and physios also came. The place was packed with standing room only. I hoped my little angel would agree we had done her proud! We never knew on this day how huge an impact she'd had on so many. She may have left, but her legacy was only just starting!

Alan struggled as much as I in dealing with the loss. The whole funeral and funeral parlour situation just felt like a process to him. He felt Livvy was being treated like a product which needed to be dealt with, completed and then someone would shout, "Next." Petty things would easily remind him, and he'd be crying at the sight of a policeman, or something on television. Sometimes we'd be walking around literally like zombies, consumed by grief. Nothing around us mattered, it all now seemed pointless.

I'd read an article about a child who had grown up having lost a sibling tragically to illness. Some words were said that affected me deeply. "On the day I lost my brother, I lost my parents also, consumed in sorrow". I researched the story further, and realised the potential danger here. We had to acknowledge our sorrow and grief, but also think hard for our other three girls. They each needed our support and had to learn it was alright to love again. The only way our girls were going to know it was ok was for them to see us doing it. I remember feeling so false. I tried to be jovial and laugh at some stupid things. I felt so fake, but then I started to see the girls smile again and I knew it was worth it! I put my own grief away in a box, and might have driven the girls mad constantly trying to make everything perfect! I was filling the empty moments doing ridiculous things like ironing underwear, because I didn't know how to be doing nothing. My three poor girls never had a minute's peace as I fussed around them!

Each girl dealt with it very differently. Kennedy was quite hard about it, with an impression, "I'm hard. I'm hard, nobody's going to hurt me again!' Eden didn't know how to process it! She didn't know if she could cry. She'd punch a wall and hurt herself and when she had physical pain, it was ok to cry. She didn't feel it was ok to cry at emotional stuff. Brodie was absolutely distraught! Her best friend had gone! They were like two peas in a pod. When Brodie went to do something, she'd realize Livvy wasn't there. The two older girls had often been in their room playing together and keeping each other company. It was mostly Brodie who had been getting toys out to play with Livvy, and it was hard now watching her take out the toys and seeing her face when she realized Livvy wasn't there anymore. Brodie had never been in the position of having to play on her own. It was so hard to see. I bought Brodie a little heart shaped necklace with the name "Livvy" on it, and she would not take it off. She refused! At school in PE they insisted she remove it, but Brodie would only do so if the teacher promised to guard it with her life. Brodie needed tangible things to touch, to ease the loss of her sister. We had a long journey to make ensuring our girls knew it was ok to laugh, love and to live again. This was now 100% my focus!

Chapter 7

We had to wait a further four weeks, after Livvy's funeral in December, before we were informed what had been the cause of Livvy's death. This was an agonising time, with a million "What if" or "If only we'd" scenarios torturing both Alan and me every hour of every day and night.

Four weeks after the funeral we attended the local hospital for the inquest into Livvy's death. It felt surreal to have gone all this time and still have no idea what had taken Livvy from us! Every possibility had been played out in our minds, every possibility except the one which was finally presented to us.

We were seated in a large conference room around a table, just wondering what was going to be said. The not knowing and having unanswered questions for nine years had almost become normality as a parent of a child with Rett. For us the unanswered question period had still further to drag on.

Present at the inquest, besides Alan and myself, was my mother in law, Brenda, and my dad, Phil. There were also, to my surprise, reporters from the local news. I hadn't expected this, but inquests are an open event, so I suppose I should have expected that anybody could turn up. The pathologist had come from Birmingham Children's Hospital, and there was also the coroner and his clerical support staff.

This might sound like a very strange thing to say, but the inquest was lovely! If you imagine how long we had waited, and how desperate we were for information, then you might appreciate what a relief it was when the answers were finally given to us. The coroner and pathologist were so nice, and so incredibly understanding and sympathetic! They went through all the things they had looked at and ruled out, and repeatedly emphasised that there was nothing we could have done which would have made any difference! They worked hard to get this point over to me, and I imagined they must have heard that I had been blaming myself. I couldn't stop questioning if there was something I should have done. Was there something I should have noticed? They took a lot of time making sure I understood that this wasn't the case.

The pathologist was a smart gentleman in his forties, wearing a smart three-piece suit. I remember even his smart gentleman's umbrella with its brown wooden handle. His hair style and spectacles gave him a very prim and proper demeanour. He was a man who clearly took immense pride in his work, and he set about explaining how difficult an investigation this had been. He went through all the Rett Syndrome related conditions that he had tested for and how he had ruled each condition out. He then explained how he had needed to go further afield making enquiries and that it was only following the results from blood culture tests that answers finally became available. I remember listening to him explaining how each test had been carried out and thinking that this was a man who loved his science. He was happy. He was, of course, not happy with investigating child death, but I could see he got immense pleasure from being able to give us the answers and explanations we so desperately craved. This was a clever, wonderful and professional man who did a job few would wish to do. He did it with fantastic ability and knew the true value of his findings and the importance in how they should be delivered with compassion, clarity and understanding.

A person with Rett will also have a weakened immune system, and Livvy, sadly, was no different. The abnormal breathing in a girl with Rett means that breathing takes more effort than it does for most people, so that left her immune system even lower. When you add to this all the medication she was taking for epilepsy, which also weakens the immune system, you can understand why she was weak. It would not be an exaggeration to say that, if Livvy was in a room and somebody sneezed, then Livvy would catch a cold.

She had developed a Streptococcal Type A infection, and this is what had finally taken her. They explained that this is not only an incredibly aggressive virus, but it can take hold extremely fast and without warning. The pathologist explained about other cases when healthier and stronger people than Livvy had succumbed to this virus while in the care of doctors who'd still not been able to save them. They gave examples which explained just how quickly this virus can do its damage. They went through the events of the night, and especially from Alan seeing her at half past one in the morning and saying his "Goodnight Treacle," through to half past four. They repeated and explained that this was more than enough time for the virus to be fatal, and that

Alan couldn't expect that he should have noticed anything untoward at that time. We had to stop blaming ourselves. This was drummed home!

The symptoms of the virus are often not visible until such a time as it's too late. It is extremely quick and deadly and has previously been known as 'Marine's Disease.' This was due to an outbreak in America in which a few Marines became ill, and, despite being under doctor's observations, some died. In this case the marines' immune systems were down because of the work rates demanded of them during training.

The coroner, also, was lovely during the inquest. He was older, in his sixties, and also wore a suit. It was not quite as dapper as the pathologist's. He talked about Livvy's life, and made a point of how well loved Livvy had been. He highlighted how she was well cared for and how good her nutrition was. He noticed tiny details, such as how her fingernails had been filed, and told us how obvious it was that Livvy had been well cared for. Things like this made a big difference to us at the time!

I didn't want a copy of the coroner's report after the inquest. I had sat crying through most of it, and I didn't feel that reading about all the tests again would do anything to help. I would just have kept going over and over it again!

I went home and processed this information. It was obvious for me that Rett had weakened Livvy's breathing and immune system, and even if not directly responsible for her death, it was certainly what had made her weak and allowed the virus to get in. I was so angry with Rett! I had a choice. I could either be consumed in anger or I could fight back. I knew what Livvy would want me to do! Also, I never wanted her name to be forgotten. Rett had stolen my child and I felt dammed if I wasn't going to try and stop it taking others! I was also very conscious of just how much Livvy loved life! Whatever we were going to do had to be about something bigger than Rett. It had to be about making the most of life. The sad reality is that there are many children who are going to have short lives. However, Livvy was a shining example of how important it is to live that short life to the full, and make each precious second count to the maximum. We had so many memories tied up, and ideas which we wanted to share. I thought back to when a doctor had first given us the diagnosis. I realized that what he had given us wasn't a burden. It was a big green flag of freedom! We had our eyes suddenly opened wide, and knew on that day, that we had to start living life, now. From that moment, we used every second, and every spare penny, to live life to the full, as a family. We can all now look back and cherish those memories with joy. As a family we now wanted to make sure other families in similar situations also had the opportunity to make their own special memories of happiness and fun, and not just of sadness and pain. It was with this goal in mind that we created the charity

www.livvyssmile.co.uk

Chapter 8, Life after Livvy

Livvy's legacy started following a family discussion, when we all sat and contributed ideas of what Livvy enjoyed most, and we thought about what would best help others. We needed a name for this and it was my youngest daughter who mentioned, "What do we think about, when we think of Livvy? Her Smiles." That was how we got the name www.livvyssmile.co.uk

We wanted to make wonderful days of memories for children with disabilities. This wasn't limited just to children with Rett Syndrome but was intended to include those with other serious disabilities also.

We set about raising funds by holding Karaoke nights in a pub in Little Bloxwich, called The Beacon Way, and selling raffle tickets until we had sufficient funds to achieve this. This was originally intended to be a one-off event. We hired the donkey sanctuary at which Livvy had experienced so much pleasure. We had the whole place to ourselves. We had all the donkeys, the staff, entertainers and even had the local fire brigade joining us, helping to create a fun day. All the children in the area who had disabilities were invited to join us. The memory- making day was not a fund-raising day. It was a day for spending funds and creating precious memories of good times. It had not been our intention to make this a regular event, but, as a family, we were blown away by just how effective it was. We loved looking at the photographs and seeing the total joy on the face of each child! This was not only an event for the disabled children, but also for their siblings. It can be hard for these children to go to parties sometimes. When you go to a party with a severely disabled child, you will always be hoping they are not going to kick off, hoping people are not going to be whispering and pointing at the weird one! My goal had been to create the safe environment in which everybody understood and nobody felt uncomfortable. I saw my very dear friend Ann-Marie's little boy, Ryan, in the photographs, with his face painted, having a fantastic day! He was enjoying it as much as he had enjoyed the camping trips with Livvy previously. It made everything so worthwhile when his mum explained afterwards how hard she also found it, to attend events and parties. She was so thankful that we'd given her a day of freedom and fun in a safe, friendly environment. Sadly, soon after the memory- making day, Ryan's condition became worse and, after a stay in hospital, he also went to sleep, never to wake up again. I only hope he is laughing and making mischief up there in Heaven with Livvy, as they both did together on the camping trip! How could we ever dream of making this a one-off event after Ann-Marie had told me how much she now cherished the memories of that day? Of course, we didn't! We repeated it numerous times, and also hired the Special Needs Adventure Playground for similar days, and held tea parties at campsites. We had Christmas parties at which the children could make their own teddy bears. They all loved putting the stuffing into their own individual bears. We went into schools and had music days, and bought toys for hospital wards with the funds we managed to raise. We wanted to make sure all kids had appropriate sensory toys while on the hospital wards. The fund raising took off with Kennedy and a friend doing cake stalls and a local school doing events to raise money. We arranged further Karaoke nights and anything we could to keep this dream going. Alan loved his radio-controlled car racing and Tamworth Radio Racing Auto Club kindly started donating the track use, for free, and we made that an event with further cake sales. This alone started raising hundreds each year. Alan had his chest waxed to raise money, and there was a sponsored run somebody else organised to help us. We were driven by the smiles and fabulous memories we were creating. This remains an ongoing passion for our whole family to this day.

I have, since the age of twelve, always wanted to foster a child. This dated back to knowing a child at school who could only be described as a nightmare for various issues. One day this boy disappeared, and nobody knew why. He eventually came back to school and nobody recognised him. I was later to learn that he had been taken from quite a bad home environment and placed into the care of a foster family. He had thrived! The change in him was unbelievable, and from that day I'd always wanted to be able to offer that gift to another child. The positive impact fostering had on that boy's life just struck me! Years later, when I met Alan, I did warn him that I wanted to have about six kids and foster hundreds more. He just laughed, thinking I was joking, but he should have listened more!

Livvy had passed away in the November and, sadly, the following Christmas was the first time ever that I had been fully organized, and I'd already bought all the presents! While I did have all the receipts, I couldn't just take them back to the shop. This just didn't feel right. How could I take the presents I'd bought for Livvy and hand them back to the shop? Instead I searched on Google and found a local children's home which, by coincidence, also looked after youngsters who had complex needs. The home, called Shire Oak, would be the perfect place to give Livvy's Christmas presents a lovely home! Alan and I went to the home and met some of the kids. They were so sweet! The manager was so sympathetic and listened to our story. She told us about the home, and I also said how much I admired what she did. She explained that they had some kids who also needed foster placement, and they were trying to find suitable families to foster children with complex needs. I said that this was something I had always wanted to do, but that now was still not the right time. It was still only December, and we were still very much in the midst of our grief. The manager said, "I understand, it isn't the right time, but if you ever feel the time is right at a later date, and this is something you want to do, please come back to Shire Oak and we can have a chat." I did think about this for a long while.

The idea of fostering sat in my mind for months. It sat in Alan's head also. One day we finally had a conversation wondering if we could ask the girls if they could go through this with us. We organised a family meeting. It was instantly obvious that all three of them were thrilled with the idea of giving another child a home, and voted a unanimous "Yes!" I wanted to help a child who had disabilities, but I didn't want to cope with life threatening disabilities. I just thought the girls had already been through so much. I couldn't imagine putting them through this! I still think that if they had brought me a child on this day who I knew was going to pass away, I would have said, "No!" I was not prepared to do that to my daughters!

We registered our interest with an independent fostering company, who then started the lengthy process which included diverse types of assessments for suitability. Eventually after all the boxes had been ticked, and assessments passed, Alan and I went to panel. I was totally bemused that Alan and I were rejected by the panel and sent away. I couldn't understand it. I later sought feedback and learned it was a paperwork misunderstanding. On Alan's form he had written that he loved to go RC racing every Friday evening, referring to his love of Radio Control Cars. The social worker did not understand what this meant and wrongly assumed he liked to go joyriding around in stolen cars on a Friday evening. Although a ridiculous error, we both couldn't help but laugh at the mistake. The owner of the foster company came and talked to us after the meeting and apologised. Fresh paperwork was then submitted.

The second visit to panel was much more, straight forward, and we were given the opportunity to foster a gorgeous fourteen-month old little boy. (Details about this boy or his conditions cannot be included within this book because he will forever be subject of a Child Protection Order.) All I can say is, he had heart problems and other very severe medical conditions. Our family had trouble caused by his family both during and after the time during which we cared for him. This little boy could be the subject of his own book but, for legal reasons, I will never be allowed to tell that story. Sadly, just after his second birthday he was watching Story Teller one afternoon at home and he just went still. Despite all our best efforts to resuscitate him, his heart was too weak and he passed away. The events of that day, such as the trip in the ambulance, waiting in the little room, the doctor coming to tell us how hard they'd tried, were all a horrific rerun of the dreadful day when Livvy had passed. It was my worst nightmare returning and having to be relived once more. It seemed so unfair that we should be sitting in that same little waiting room again, and getting the same experience, but with one very traumatic difference. I knew, when we got our chance to see his tiny body and give our last hugs, that it was "Goodbye" there and then. He was no longer our little boy, and we would have no say in any decisions relating to him. The family who had caused us such problems were also not going to allow us to attend his funeral! My fragile heart was shattered again as I left the hospital, only to return once more to a house full of police officers conducting their routine investigations while I cried my eyes out. It was extremely hard for my girls because none of them had the chance to say "Good bye." We also didn't go to the inquest because of threats we'd received, and even the police told us that it would be a bad idea, and recommended we stay away. We did our own private thing as a family to remember that amazing young man whose story I will never be able to share!

In the depths of grief, I felt guilty for being selfish and fostering to fill my own needs. It had been a terrible mistake! I couldn't believe what I had put everyone through, and promised them I'd never put them through anything like this ever again. My nine year-old youngest daughter, Brodie saw things very differently, and demanded a family meeting. I was being called out by my nine-year-old. Brodie said "If we hadn't been brave after Livvy's death, then this little boy would never have known love. The love he had experienced was part of Livvy's legacy. If we don't become brave once more, what kind of legacy does that leave for him?" Brodie called me out by reminding me how we'd taught them to live life by making moments magical and loving hard now, and not worrying about the future. She was, of course, correct. My wise little owl!

In January 2011 we fostered another slightly older boy through Progress Care Solutions. This was an eight-year-old, who had a combination of both behaviour issues and related medical issues. He is also subject to a Child Protection Order, and his story also can't be shared within this book for legal reasons. He came as a very quiet and detached little boy, and he has transformed into a social butterfly who now knows himself. There are few things more rewarding than helping a child discover himself and gain confidence in his own personality and know he's loved. While I can't give further details about this young man, I can say that he has continued to thrive into his teenage years, and is enjoying many magic family moments still to this day.

In December 2016 we had a phone call about another tiny little boy called Daniel, needing respite care. He was 16 months old and also had complex medical needs. These included multi-pituitary hormone deficiency, hydrocephalus, diabetes insipidus, cerebral palsy, hypothalamic dysfunction and epilepsy, and he was also blind. I didn't even know what all these conditions were! I knew he was gastro fed using a tube to his stomach, which was something I knew we could do. I almost said "No." I don't like the idea of emergency respite, because it breaks my heart when I must give them back. I like to spend time with a child. I like to invest my time in a child. I know there are some incredible respite foster parents who do amazing things but this just isn't for me. However, I homed in on the epilepsy and the feeding and thought, why not? This is something I could help with. A family meeting was held and another unanimous "Yes" vote decided Daniel would be joining us. Nobody said "Yes" quicker than Alan. His words were "We're doing this one. It will do us good. It will be a fun weekend." To this day each time Daniel wakes us up in the night, I still tease him saying "You said 'Yes'!"

He turned up on the Friday night with his foster parents and, quite predictably, I fell in love with this child straight away. My heart just says "There's another place there. Jump in." Sunday came, and, predictably, we felt very sad having to return him. We forgot an item of equipment, so I did get to see him again on the Monday when I returned it.

The foster company then called us and asked how things had gone, and I told them we thought Daniel was adorable. This pleased them, and they offered us the opportunity to do regular respite. I had to refuse, which surprised them after I'd said he was adorable. I explained how upset the whole family had been having to return Daniel on the Sunday evening. The girls had also become very attached and cried when we'd had to return him. I had to tell the agency that we no longer wanted to do respite fostering because we wouldn't want to give them back. This was a rule I felt we needed to stick to, for our own piece of mind.

Not long after this I was Christmas shopping and I received a further phone call from the foster company. They said "You know when you said you didn't want to do respite fostering? How would you feel about having Daniel on a long-term placement?"

I said "Yes", in a heartbeat. I had to check with Alan and the girls first, so I rang them. The immediate response was "Yes, yes phone them back, phone them back. What are you calling us for?"

We agreed to have Daniel, and we were so excited he was coming back! The day of his arrival finally came on

29th December 2016. The social worker arrived with loads of bags and boxes and all his things, but no Daniel. I asked, "Where's Daniel?"

"Sorry, he's in the children's hospital ill," was the response.

We were straight over to the hospital, where he spent the next nine days, having developed some complications around his medical conditions. This, in a very strange way, was a funny sort of blessing, because it allowed us to spend days with him, surrounded by the medical support he needed. We had the opportunity to pump the specialists for knowledge about all his conditions and learn exactly what was needed to keep him healthy, when the time should come for us to be taking him home. The time did come in early January, and we were so happy to have him back in our family. I need to mention that Daniel didn't end up in foster care because he had a bad mother or any type of abuse. It was simply a matter that his mother was very young and he had incredibly complex medical needs, which would have been too much for many people to cope with, let alone a very young mother. She is a beautiful young lady who was and still is very much involved in Daniel's life, and having visits. She loves him deeply still, and she absolutely tried her best!

Daniel thrived and developed amazingly considering the difficulties he faces and he is the most outstanding, gorgeous, loving little boy. When he was later offered up for permanent adoption a huge chunk of my faith was restored. I knew that this lovely little boy had done so much to enrich the quality of my family's life and God wanted me to look after him. Alan and I had no hesitation adopting Daniel, and we relished the opportunity to fill each day with as many magic moments as possible, as we do for our other children. This was completed and finalised on 27th June 2017 which is why I can talk now about Daniel in this book in a way I can't about the other boys I've fostered.

Livvy was the gift which just kept on giving. She changed us. We took life for granted until we had Livvy. She is the motivation in everything I do for other children, and for other parents. I am a fighter for disabled rights. I do that, because of Livvy. There were so many things that followed Livvy's passing which must also remain part of her legacy. I remember thinking, how sad I felt, and I uploaded a picture with the hashtag #NoMoreEmptyArms and #RettSyndrome and this went viral. I received messages of support from all over the world and interest from the local news. Brodie was given an award for the work she has put in, and had the opportunity to meet Prince Harry. He asked, "Why do you do all this?"

Brodie could only reply "Because she's my sister!"

Even this book itself is part of Livvy's legacy, and all profits will be going to help find a cure for this devastating condition. In 2007 scientists found a way to reverse the condition in mice, and hopes were raised enormously. Raising the money to continue this brilliant work has only been possible due to the fantastic dedicated fund raisers and scientists who have worked tirelessly ever since. The reality is that two huge milestones are set to be achieved in the very near future. One thing which makes Rett a life shortening condition for many is the breathing abnormality it causes. Effective drugs and treatments for this are already in the initial stages of testing and this will give thousands of girls a greater life expectancy, if successful. More excitingly, the drugs and treatment programmes looking at reversing Rett Syndrome are getting closer each day. We are awaiting an announcement any day from Bio-tech Company AveXis about human gene therapy clinical trials which will hopefully take place in 2018. The potential cure has never been closer. This is an outrageously expensive treatment, but each of these beautiful angels deserves the chance of a return to full life!

An American website described Rett Syndrome perfectly by explaining "It's like having Cerebral Palsy, Epilepsy, Autism and Parkinson's disease all rolled into one. If you can picture this, you are close to understanding the horror these girls endure. You don't just have the problems with the joints. You don't just have epilepsy. You don't just have breathing problems. You don't just have feeding issues. You don't just have communication issues. You have them all."

NOTES FROM THE AUTHOR:

The below are a few of Sara Meredith's own special words about Livvy:

I tried hard to listen as I sat there in the doctor's office.

Yet all I could hear were the words, "She cannot" or

"She won't be able to."

It was as if the diagnosis had defined the rest of my

daughter's life for her. Leaving her with nothing to achieve

or experience.

Thankfully the doctor may have known the syndrome

but they did not know my daughter.

"Never say never" became our family motto and my

goodness, did that girl live it!

I'm sure she took a mental list of what the doctors said

that day, all those things they said she couldn't do

became her targets, her goals.

She didn't let us in on her secret, just surprised us each time

when she defied the odds.

I loved watching the faces of those surprised.

"She won't walk again" became "Oh my goodness she is

walking."

"She won't eat solids again" became "Pass her the burger."

It was never about her weakness, her inner strength

made sure of that.

A person should not be defined by their disability.

We never look at the limits but look to the possibilities.

It's about "Never saying never," as who really knows?

I left the doctor's office with the sound of defeat in my ears.

My daughter left with the same sheer will

that had kept her fighting for so long.

We learned the words "We cannot" were to be

banned from our vocabulary.

We replaced them with "How shall we?"

Camping, rock climbing, ice skating are never words

we associate with a child in a wheelchair yet my

girl, she achieved them all.

Higher is better and faster is certainly more fun.

Life was to be lived that is for sure.

Best friends, boyfriends, and how many nights did

I cry myself to sleep believing these were never to be

for my daughter.

Yes, she had them all.

Her smile and mischievous nature won hearts wherever

she went.

Doctors were speechless, dreams were again to be dreamed.

Inspirational, determined, pure stubborn that was my girl.

This little lady showed us that courage has no bounds.

That with sheer will and determination amazing things can be achieved.

"Never say never." Our girl never did.

Livvy's Legacy
Written by Dr Alison Britland - Paediatrician

Living with a child who has a severe disability must be devastating for any family, living with a child who has an undiagnosed severe disability must be even worse, and living with a child who has an undiagnosed progressive neurodegenerative condition must be unspeakably difficult. To watch your beloved daughter, lose a little bit of herself every day is a heart –wrenching, soul- destroying torture. What is so remarkable about this account is that it's not primarily focused on the family's suffering or even Livvy's suffering but instead is written in honour of the person she was.

Not Livvy the Rett's child, but Livvy the much-cherished daughter who just happened to have Rett's.

Many but by no means all children with a disability have a specific recognisable collection of symptoms and signs which enable Paediatricians to reach a timely diagnosis. Accurate information helps the child and her family to move forward with a clear picture of what lies ahead. This is much more difficult if the child has a rare condition which even an experienced Paediatrician may not have come across. Over many years as a Consultant Acute Paediatrician I can only recall 4 children with a diagnosis of Rett's so it's not surprising that obtaining a name for their daughter's condition took some time, unfortunately adding to the family's distress.

Sadly, even after diagnosis for some conditions there is still no prospect of a cure or even a slowing down of the disease's progression. Rett's syndrome is different however- there is a very real prospect of managing this disease in the future, perhaps even amounting to a cure which would be truly amazing. Funding for well known conditions is much more readily available than for those equally well deserving but rarer such as Rett's.

This is why Livvy's story is not only inspirational but hugely important. If the family can raise awareness and funds through the sale of this book, then the prospect of a cure is that little bit closer.

Livvy's mum should be very proud of having had the courage to tell her story. But most of all she should be very proud of having been Livvy's mum.

See more at www.livvyssmile.co.uk

If you would like to help a little more than just buying this book and help make Rett Syndrome a thing of the past, then please donate at www.reverserett.org.uk and spread the word. Every donation can make a difference. Thank you!

Find out more about the author Andre Govier on Facebook. Or on Twitter at https://twitter.com/Andregovier

Please if you think this book will help others leave a review on www.Amazon.com

Made in the USA
Monee, IL
19 February 2023

28280442R00075